HOW
Build a PC

MASTER GUIDE

FOR COMPLETE

Copyright © 2024 by Doug Williams

All rights reserved. No part of this publication may be reproduced, distributed, or transmitted in any form or by any means. This includes photocopying, recording, or any mechanical methods, without the prior written permission of the publisher. Brief quotations embodied in reviews and certain other noncommercial uses permitted by copyright law.

Chapter 1: Introduction to Building Your Own Computer	**12**
Benefits of Building Over Buying	12
Common Myths and Misconceptions	14
Tools and Safety Equipment Needed	16
A Roadmap to Success	17
Chapter 2: How Computers Work	**19**
A Simplified Explanation of How Computer Components Interact	19
The Core Functions: Input, Output, Processing, and Storage	21
The Interaction Between Components: A Practical Example	23
Why This Matters for Building a PC	24
Chapter 3: Choosing Your Purpose	**25**
The Four Primary Build Types	25
Balancing Performance, Budget, and Future-Proofing	29
Final Thoughts	30
Chapter 4: The CPU (Central Processing Unit)	**31**
What the CPU Does	31
Differences Between Intel and AMD Processors	33
Selecting a CPU Based on Your Needs	34
Future-Proofing Your CPU Choice	36
Final Thoughts	37
Chapter 5: The Motherboard	**38**
The Role of the Motherboard in a Computer Build	38
Compatibility: The Foundation of a Successful Build	39
Understanding Form Factors	41
Features to Look For in a Motherboard	42
Final Thoughts	44
Chapter 6: RAM (Random Access Memory)	**45**
What RAM Does and Why It Matters	45
Differences in Speed, Size, and DDR Versions	46
How Much RAM Is Needed for Different Tasks	48

Choosing RAM for Your Build 50
A Key Element of Your Build 50

Chapter 7: Storage Options: HDD, SSD, and NVMe Drives 52

The Importance of Storage Speed and Capacity 52
Comparing HDDs, SATA SSDs, and NVMe SSDs 54
Choosing the Right Drive for Your Build 56
Maximizing Your Storage Setup 58
The Building Blocks of Data 58

Chapter 8: The GPU (Graphics Processing Unit) 60

What the GPU Does and When You Need a Dedicated One 60
Nvidia vs. AMD GPUs 62
How to Pick a GPU for Gaming, Video Editing, or 3D Rendering 63
Balancing Performance and Budget 66
Enhancing Your Build with the Right GPU 67

Chapter 9: The Power Supply Unit (PSU) 68

Why a Reliable PSU Is Crucial 68
Calculating Your Power Needs 69
Understanding PSU Ratings (80 Plus, Bronze, Gold) 71
How to Choose the Right PSU 72
Investing in Stability and Longevity 74

Chapter 10: The Case 75

Choosing a Case Based on Size, Cooling, and Aesthetics 75
Popular Case Brands and Features 77
Managing Airflow and Cable Organization 79
The Case as Your Build's Foundation 81

Chapter 11: Cooling Systems 82

Air Cooling vs. Liquid Cooling 82
Choosing a CPU Cooler: Stock vs. Aftermarket 84
Case Fan Setups for Optimal Airflow 87
Keeping Your Build Cool and Efficient 88

Chapter 12: Peripherals: Monitors, Keyboards, and Mice 90
    Choosing Peripherals to Match Your Build   90
    Overview of Monitor Types   91
    Gaming vs. Productivity-Focused Peripherals   93
    Creating the Perfect Setup   96
Chapter 13: Operating Systems and Software   97
    Windows, Linux, or macOS?   97
    How to Obtain and Install an Operating System   100
    Essential Software for a New PC   102
    Your Operating System, Your Control   104
Chapter 14: Setting a Budget   105
    Allocating Your Budget Across Components   105
    Prioritizing Upgrades and Where to Spend   107
    Tips for Maximizing Your Budget   110
    Smart Spending for a Balanced Build   111
Chapter 15: Where to Buy Components   112
    Reliable Websites and Stores   112
    Tips for Finding Deals and Avoiding Scams   115
    Considerations for Used Parts   116
    Smart Shopping for a Successful Build   118
Chapter 16: Compatibility and Building Tools   120
    Using PCPartPicker to Plan Your Build   120
    Understanding Compatibility Checks   122
    Essential Tools for Assembly   124
    Preparing Your Workspace   126
    Building with Confidence   126
Chapter 17: Preparing Your Workspace   128
    Setting Up a Static-Free Environment   128
    Organizing Your Components and Tools   130
    Preparing the Case   131
    Create a Comfortable Environment   132
    The Perfect Workspace for a Stress-Free Build   133
Chapter 18: Step-by-Step Assembly   134

Step 1: Installing the CPU and Cooler 134
Step 2: Mounting the Motherboard in the Case 135
Step 3: Inserting RAM and Storage Drives 136
Step 4: Connecting the Power Supply and GPU 138
Double-Check Your Work 139
A Complete System 139
Chapter 19: Cable Management **141**
Why Cable Management Matters 141
How to Keep Cables Organized for Better Airflow 142
Tips for Using Zip Ties and Velcro Straps 143
Tools and Accessories for Cable Management 145
Final Touches for a Clean Build 146
Effort Pays Off 147
Chapter 20: First Boot and BIOS Setup **148**
First Boot: Checking for a Successful Boot-Up 148
Navigating the BIOS to Check Hardware Recognition 150
Updating the BIOS for Better Stability 151
Troubleshooting First Boot Issues 152
The Foundation of Your Build 153
Chapter 21: Installing Your Operating System **154**
How to Boot from a USB Drive 154
Step-by-Step Guide to Installing Windows 155
Step-by-Step Guide to Installing Linux 157
Setting Up Drivers for Optimal Performance 158
Testing Your System 160
A Fully Functional System 160
Chapter 22: Optimization and Maintenance **162**
Overclocking Basics for CPU and GPU 162
Keeping Your System Cool and Dust-Free 165
Tips for Troubleshooting Common Problems 166
Keeping Your PC in Top Shape 168

Chapter 1: Introduction to Building Your Own Computer

Building your own computer can seem like a daunting task, especially if you're new to the world of hardware. However, the rewards of creating a custom PC tailored to your specific needs far outweigh the initial intimidation. This chapter is your first step on the journey, offering an introduction to the benefits of building over buying, debunking common myths and misconceptions, and outlining the tools and safety equipment needed to ensure a smooth and successful build.

Benefits of Building Over Buying

When most people think about purchasing a computer, their first instinct is to head to a store or browse online for pre-assembled options. While buying a pre-built machine might seem like the easiest path, building your own computer offers numerous advantages that make it worth considering.

1. Cost Efficiency

Building your own PC often saves you money in the long run. Pre-built computers include added costs for assembly, branding, and often unnecessary features. By selecting your own components, you ensure every dollar is spent on performance rather than overhead. For example:

- **Customizable Budget:** You can prioritize spending on critical parts like the CPU or GPU and save on non-essentials.
- **Avoiding Bloatware:** Pre-built systems often come with unnecessary software that can slow down your computer and waste resources.

2. Customization

Building a PC allows you to design a system that meets your exact needs. Whether you're a gamer, content creator, or casual user, you can select components that optimize performance for your intended tasks. Key areas of customization include:

- **Hardware Specifications:** Choose the exact CPU, GPU, RAM, and storage that suit your needs.
- **Aesthetics:** Customize your PC's case, lighting, and fans to reflect your personal style.
- **Upgradability:** A custom-built PC makes it easier to replace or upgrade parts in the future without being locked into proprietary components.

3. Performance

When you build your own computer, you control its performance capabilities. Pre-built machines often sacrifice quality to hit price points, bundling low-end parts where it's harder for consumers to notice. With a custom build, you can:

- Ensure high-quality components for better reliability.
- Optimize cooling and airflow for peak performance.
- Overclock the CPU or GPU for additional power.

4. Education and Empowerment

The process of building your own PC provides a deeper understanding of how computers work. Once you've built one, you'll find troubleshooting, upgrading, and maintaining your system far less intimidating. You'll gain:

- **Knowledge of Components:** Learn how each part functions and contributes to the system.
- **Confidence in Problem-Solving:** Feel empowered to fix issues instead of relying on expensive tech support.

Common Myths and Misconceptions

Despite its advantages, many people shy away from building their own PC due to common myths. Let's debunk these to ease any concerns you might have.

Myth 1: Building a Computer Is Too Difficult

One of the biggest misconceptions is that building a computer requires extensive technical expertise. While it's true that the process involves some learning, most modern components are designed to be user-friendly. For example:

- **Components Are Modular:** Parts like RAM, GPUs, and CPUs are designed to slot into place easily.
- **Online Resources Are Plentiful:** Websites, forums, and video tutorials provide step-by-step guidance.

Myth 2: I Might Damage the Components

It's natural to worry about breaking expensive parts, but with proper care and precautions, the risk is minimal. Techniques like grounding yourself to prevent static electricity and handling components gently are straightforward and effective.

Myth 3: Pre-Built Computers Are Always Better

While pre-built machines may be convenient, they rarely offer the best value or performance for the price. Custom PCs typically outpace pre-built ones in terms of longevity and power, especially when tailored to specific uses.

Myth 4: Building a Computer Is Time-Consuming

Many people imagine that assembling a computer takes days, but most builds can be completed in just a few hours, even by beginners. The planning phase, such as selecting parts, may take time, but the assembly itself is quicker than most expect.

Myth 5: It's Hard to Find the Right Parts

Thanks to tools like **PCPartPicker** (which checks for compatibility among components), selecting the right parts is easier than ever. Detailed reviews and guides online also help simplify decision-making.

Tools and Safety Equipment Needed

Now that we've dispelled the myths, let's focus on preparing for your build. Having the right tools and understanding basic safety precautions will make the process smoother and stress-free.

1. Tools for Assembly

Building a computer doesn't require a full toolbox. A few basic tools are sufficient:

- **Screwdriver Set:** A magnetic Phillips-head screwdriver is essential for securing components. Some screws may require smaller sizes, so having a set with multiple sizes is helpful.
- **Anti-Static Wrist Strap:** This inexpensive tool prevents static electricity from damaging sensitive components.

- **Cable Ties or Velcro Straps:** Used for cable management to keep wires organized and improve airflow.
- **Thermal Paste:** If your CPU cooler doesn't come with pre-applied thermal paste, you'll need a small tube to ensure proper heat transfer.
- **Flashlight:** Helpful for working in tight spaces or poorly lit areas.

2. Workspace Setup

Creating the right environment is crucial for a safe and efficient build:

- **Static-Free Area:** Work on a wooden or tiled surface rather than carpet to reduce static buildup. Touch a metal object or wear an anti-static wrist strap before handling parts.
- **Clean Surface:** Clear your workspace of clutter to avoid losing small screws or components.
- **Comfortable Lighting:** Ensure your workspace is well-lit to prevent mistakes.

3. Safety Precautions

- **Handle Components Carefully:** Always hold components by their edges and avoid touching the metal contacts.
- **Ground Yourself:** Use an anti-static wrist strap or periodically touch a grounded metal object to discharge static electricity.

- **Avoid Rushing:** Take your time to follow instructions and double-check your work to prevent errors.

A Roadmap to Success

By the end of this book, you'll not only have a functional custom PC but also a deeper appreciation for how computers work. Whether your goal is to build a powerful gaming rig, a reliable workstation, or a versatile home computer, the journey starts here.

In the next chapter, we'll dive into the inner workings of a computer, providing a foundational understanding of how each component interacts. Armed with this knowledge, you'll feel even more confident as you start selecting the parts for your build.

Let's get started!

Chapter 2: How Computers Work

Understanding how a computer works is essential before diving into building your own. At its core, a computer is a collection of components that interact seamlessly to perform a wide range of tasks, from browsing the web to rendering complex 3D models. This chapter offers a simplified explanation of how these components work together and provides an overview of the core functions: input, output, processing, and storage.

A Simplified Explanation of How Computer Components Interact

At its most basic level, a computer takes in data (input), processes that data, stores it if necessary, and then delivers a result (output). These tasks rely on the harmonious interaction of several key components, each playing a distinct role. Let's break down how these components work together in a simplified, step-by-step manner:

Step 1: Powering the System

The **Power Supply Unit (PSU)** is the unsung hero of any computer. It converts electricity from your wall outlet into usable power for all components. Without the PSU, nothing else in your system can function. The PSU distributes this power to components like the CPU, motherboard, GPU, and storage devices.

Step 2: Processing Data

The **Central Processing Unit (CPU)** acts as the "brain" of the computer. It performs calculations, executes commands, and processes data. When you run an application, the CPU interprets the instructions and carries them out. It works closely with:

- **RAM (Random Access Memory):** A type of temporary storage that holds data the CPU needs immediately. This allows the CPU to access information quickly without constantly pulling from slower storage drives.

Step 3: Handling Graphics

If your task involves visual elements—such as gaming or video editing—the **Graphics Processing Unit (GPU)** steps in. The GPU specializes in rendering images and handling visual data more efficiently than the CPU alone.

Step 4: Storing Information

Your computer stores information using storage devices:

- **HDD (Hard Disk Drive):** A traditional, slower storage option with large capacity.
- **SSD (Solid-State Drive):** A faster storage option for quick access to files and programs.
- **NVMe Drives:** Even faster than SSDs, these are ideal for high-performance systems.

These devices keep your operating system, applications, and personal files safe for long-term use.

Step 5: Input and Output

The computer interacts with you through input and output devices:

- **Input Devices:** These include your keyboard, mouse, microphone, or game controller. They send data to the computer for processing.
- **Output Devices:** These include monitors, speakers, or printers. They display or project the results of the computer's processes.

The Core Functions: Input, Output, Processing, and Storage

To better understand how computers work, let's explore these core functions in more detail:

1. Input: How Computers Receive Information

Input devices allow you to communicate with your computer by providing data or commands. For example:

- **Typing on a Keyboard:** Sends text data to the computer.
- **Clicking with a Mouse:** Sends positional data, allowing you to navigate software.

- **Speaking into a Microphone:** Sends audio data for applications like voice recognition.

Once the input is received, the data moves through the system to the CPU for processing.

---

2. Processing: The Brain of the Operation

Processing is where the "thinking" happens. The CPU performs billions of calculations per second to interpret and execute your commands. This involves:

- **Arithmetic Logic Unit (ALU):** Handles mathematical operations.
- **Control Unit:** Directs data flow between components.
- **Cache Memory:** Stores frequently used data for rapid access.

The speed and efficiency of processing depend on your CPU's capabilities, including its clock speed (measured in GHz) and number of cores.

---

3. Storage: Keeping Your Data Safe

Computers store data in two primary ways:

- **Volatile Memory (RAM):** Temporary storage that clears when the computer is powered off. It allows the CPU to quickly access data while working.

- **Non-Volatile Memory (HDD, SSD):** Long-term storage for files, programs, and the operating system.

Data is stored as binary code (1s and 0s), which the computer interprets to represent everything from text to images and videos.

---

4. Output: Delivering Results

Once the computer processes your input, it produces an output. Examples include:

- **Displaying a Document:** Your monitor shows the processed data from a word processor.
- **Playing Music:** Your speakers project audio data processed by the CPU.
- **Printing a File:** Your printer converts digital data into a physical document.

The efficiency and quality of output depend on your output devices and the software controlling them.

The Interaction Between Components: A Practical Example

Let's take a practical example to visualize how these components interact:

1. **You press a key on your keyboard (input).**

- The keyboard sends an electrical signal representing the key to the CPU.
2. **The CPU processes the input.**
   - The CPU interprets the signal and determines the corresponding character (e.g., "A").
3. **The GPU displays the character.**
   - The GPU helps render the character on your monitor, ensuring it appears smoothly.
4. **The data is stored if needed.**
   - If you're typing in a word processor, the text may be saved temporarily in RAM or permanently on an SSD.

Why This Matters for Building a PC

Understanding how these components work together is vital for building a computer because:

- **You'll Know What to Prioritize:** For instance, if you need fast processing, you'll invest in a powerful CPU and sufficient RAM.
- **You Can Troubleshoot:** Recognizing how data flows through the system makes it easier to diagnose and fix issues.
- **You'll Build with Confidence:** Knowing the purpose of each part helps you assemble them correctly and efficiently.

In the next chapter, we'll dive deeper into the **CPU (Central Processing Unit),** exploring its role in more detail and how to select the right one for your build.

Chapter 3: Choosing Your Purpose

Building a computer is as much about understanding your needs as it is about assembling the parts. The type of PC you create depends on how you plan to use it. Are you a gamer chasing high frame rates, a content creator editing videos or rendering animations, an office worker needing a reliable setup, or someone looking for a versatile, all-purpose machine? This chapter will guide you through optimizing your build for various purposes, balancing performance with your budget, and planning for future upgrades.

The Four Primary Build Types

Every build begins with a purpose. Knowing what you want to achieve with your PC helps determine where to focus your budget and which components to prioritize.

Gaming Builds: The Graphics Powerhouse

For gamers, performance is everything. A gaming PC needs to deliver smooth, high-quality graphics, fast load times, and the ability to handle resource-intensive games without stuttering.

Key Components for Gamers

- The **GPU (Graphics Processing Unit)** is your top priority. It's the muscle behind the visuals, rendering everything from breathtaking open-world environments to fast-paced action scenes. Invest in a high-performance GPU from brands like Nvidia (GeForce RTX series) or AMD (Radeon RX series).
- A **capable CPU** ensures your GPU isn't held back. A mid-range to high-end processor with strong single-core performance, such as an Intel Core i5/i7 or AMD Ryzen 5/7, is ideal.
- **RAM** is crucial for smooth gaming. Start with at least 16GB to handle modern games, multitasking, and background processes.
- Fast storage, like an **SSD** or **NVMe drive**, significantly reduces game load times and improves overall system responsiveness.

Gamers often look for cases with excellent cooling systems and flashy aesthetics, such as RGB lighting, to enhance their setup's visual appeal.

Content Creation Builds: The Productivity Beast

If you're editing videos, creating digital art, or rendering 3D models, your PC needs to be optimized for demanding workloads. A content creation build emphasizes multitasking, speed, and reliability.

Key Components for Creators

- The **CPU** is the star player in a content creation build. Tasks like video rendering, animation, or compiling code thrive on CPUs with multiple cores and threads. Look for high-performance options like the AMD Ryzen 9 or Intel Core i9.
- **RAM** is equally important. For handling large files and running multiple applications, aim for 32GB or more.
- A **dedicated GPU** is essential for tasks like 3D rendering or working with advanced visual effects. Nvidia's RTX series or AMD's Radeon Pro cards are strong options.
- **High-capacity SSDs** are a must for storing and accessing large files quickly. Consider pairing an NVMe SSD for active projects with a traditional HDD for archival storage.

Additionally, creators should invest in a color-accurate monitor to ensure that their work looks consistent across devices.

Office Builds: The Efficient Workhorse

An office PC doesn't need to break speed records, but it should be dependable, quiet, and efficient. Whether it's for spreadsheets, emails, or virtual meetings, simplicity is key.

Key Components for Office Use

- A **budget-friendly CPU** with integrated graphics is often sufficient. Look for processors like the Intel Core i3/i5 or AMD Ryzen 3/5 with integrated GPUs.
- **8GB to 16GB of RAM** will handle everyday office tasks and light multitasking with ease.
- A **small SSD** (256GB or 512GB) ensures fast boot times and responsive applications.
- Quiet operation is critical in office environments, so choose a case with sound-dampening features and efficient cooling.

Office builds prioritize reliability over raw performance, making them cost-effective and straightforward to assemble.

General-Purpose Builds: The All-Rounder

If your PC will serve a mix of functions—light gaming, media streaming, web browsing, and office work—you'll want a general-purpose build. These versatile systems strike a balance between performance and affordability.

Key Components for Versatility

- A **mid-range CPU** with solid multitasking capabilities ensures the system can handle a variety of tasks smoothly.
- **Integrated graphics** or an entry-level dedicated GPU can manage light gaming and video streaming.
- **16GB of RAM** provides a buffer for multitasking while keeping the system responsive.

- Pairing a **500GB SSD** for the operating system with a **1TB HDD** for additional storage offers both speed and capacity.

General-purpose builds often aim for flexibility, leaving room for future upgrades to cater to changing needs.

Balancing Performance, Budget, and Future-Proofing

Building a PC involves juggling three major factors: performance, budget, and future-proofing. Striking the right balance ensures you get the best value for your money while leaving room for potential upgrades.

Start with a Budget

Your budget is the foundation of your build. Instead of splurging on one component, divide your spending strategically:

- Prioritize components that are harder to upgrade later, like the CPU and motherboard.
- Save money on items like RAM or storage, which can be expanded more easily down the line.

Think About Future Upgrades

Your PC doesn't need to be perfect on day one. Plan ahead by:

- Choosing a motherboard with additional RAM slots and support for newer CPUs.
- Selecting a power supply with extra wattage to accommodate future hardware upgrades.
- Opting for a spacious case to fit larger GPUs or additional cooling systems.

Avoid Overkill

It's easy to get swept up in the excitement of high-end components, but don't spend more than you need. If you're building an office PC, there's no reason to buy a top-tier GPU. Similarly, gamers who don't play the latest titles may not need cutting-edge hardware.

Final Thoughts

Choosing your purpose is the most important step in building your computer. It sets the direction for every decision you make, from component selection to budget allocation. By understanding what you want your PC to achieve, you're already on the path to creating a system that's perfectly tailored to your needs.

In the next chapter, we'll delve into the **CPU (Central Processing Unit)**—the heart of any computer—and learn how to choose the right processor for your build.

Chapter 4: The CPU (Central Processing Unit)

The Central Processing Unit (CPU) is often referred to as the "brain" of a computer, and for good reason. It handles nearly all the instructions and calculations required for the system to operate, making it a cornerstone of any build. In this chapter, we'll explore what the CPU does, compare the two main competitors in the market—Intel and AMD—and provide guidance on selecting the right CPU for your needs.

What the CPU Does

At its core, the CPU is responsible for executing instructions that make your computer function. Every action you take—whether it's opening a program, browsing the web, or playing a game—requires the CPU to process instructions.

How the CPU Works

The CPU operates in three main steps:

1. **Fetch:** The CPU retrieves instructions from the system's memory.
2. **Decode:** It translates these instructions into a language it can understand.

3. **Execute:** The CPU carries out the instructions, often coordinating with other components like the GPU, RAM, or storage.

This process occurs billions of times per second, allowing your computer to perform complex tasks with remarkable speed.

Key Characteristics of CPUs

Understanding these characteristics helps you evaluate a CPU's performance:

- **Clock Speed:** Measured in gigahertz (GHz), this indicates how many cycles a CPU can complete in one second. A higher clock speed generally means faster performance for single-threaded tasks.
- **Cores and Threads:** Modern CPUs have multiple cores, each capable of executing tasks independently. Threads are virtual cores created by technologies like Hyper-Threading (Intel) or Simultaneous Multi-Threading (AMD). More cores and threads enable better multitasking and improved performance in applications that support parallel processing.
- **Cache:** CPUs use a small amount of high-speed memory called cache to store frequently used data. Larger caches help reduce the time needed to retrieve data.
- **Integrated Graphics:** Some CPUs come with built-in graphics processing capabilities, eliminating the need for a dedicated GPU in low-power or budget builds.

Differences Between Intel and AMD Processors

The CPU market is dominated by two companies: Intel and AMD. Both offer powerful processors, but they differ in architecture, performance, and pricing. Here's what sets them apart:

Intel CPUs

- **Strengths:**
    - High single-core performance, which is crucial for gaming and applications that don't utilize multiple cores effectively.
    - Excellent power efficiency, especially in laptops and small form-factor PCs.
    - Reliable integrated graphics (Intel UHD or Iris Xe), making them a good choice for builds without a dedicated GPU.
- **Weaknesses:**
    - Historically more expensive than AMD CPUs for similar performance.
    - Fewer cores and threads at comparable price points, which can limit multitasking and productivity performance.

Intel's popular CPU lines include the **Core i3, i5, i7, and i9** series, with higher numbers offering better performance.

AMD CPUs

- **Strengths:**
  - More cores and threads at lower price points, making AMD ideal for multitasking and applications like video editing, rendering, and streaming.
  - Strong performance in multi-core workloads thanks to their Ryzen series processors.
  - Competitive integrated graphics in their Ryzen G-series APUs (Accelerated Processing Units).
- **Weaknesses:**
  - Slightly lower single-core performance compared to Intel in some applications, though the gap has narrowed significantly.
  - Higher power consumption in certain models, which can generate more heat.

AMD's **Ryzen 3, 5, 7, and 9** series offer tiered performance levels similar to Intel's Core lineup.

Selecting a CPU Based on Your Needs

Choosing the right CPU depends on what you plan to do with your computer. Here's how to match a CPU to your purpose:

1. Gaming

- **What Matters Most:** Single-core performance and a moderate number of cores (4–6).
- **Why:** Most modern games rely heavily on a few cores, prioritizing fast clock speeds and strong single-threaded performance.
- **Recommended CPUs:**
    - Intel Core i5 or i7 (12th or 13th generation, such as the i5-12600K or i7-13700K).
    - AMD Ryzen 5 or Ryzen 7 (5000 or 7000 series, like the Ryzen 5 5600X or Ryzen 7 7700X).

2. Content Creation

- **What Matters Most:** Multi-core performance and high thread counts.
- **Why:** Video editing, 3D rendering, and other demanding tasks benefit from CPUs with many cores and threads to handle parallel processing.
- **Recommended CPUs:**
    - Intel Core i9 (e.g., i9-13900K) for professional workloads.
    - AMD Ryzen 9 (e.g., Ryzen 9 7900X) for exceptional multi-core performance.

3. Office and Everyday Use

- **What Matters Most:** Affordability and integrated graphics.

- **Why:** Basic tasks like browsing, document editing, and video conferencing don't require powerful CPUs or dedicated GPUs.
- **Recommended CPUs:**
    - Intel Core i3 or i5 (12th generation or newer, like the i3-12100 or i5-12400).
    - AMD Ryzen 3 or Ryzen 5 (5000 series, such as the Ryzen 5 5600G with integrated graphics).

---

4. General-Purpose Builds

- **What Matters Most:** A balanced CPU that handles a bit of everything.
- **Why:** For light gaming, streaming, and multitasking, a mid-tier CPU with decent single- and multi-core performance is ideal.
- **Recommended CPUs:**
    - Intel Core i5 or i7.
    - AMD Ryzen 5 or Ryzen 7.

Future-Proofing Your CPU Choice

Technology evolves quickly, and while it's impossible to completely future-proof a system, you can take steps to extend your CPU's relevance:

1. **Opt for Newer Generations:** CPUs from the latest generation often include architectural

improvements, energy efficiency, and compatibility with faster memory or storage options.
2. **Ensure Upgrade Compatibility:** Choose a motherboard with a socket and chipset that will support future CPU upgrades (e.g., AMD's AM5 platform or Intel's LGA1700 socket).
3. **Consider More Cores:** Even if your current applications don't require many cores, future software may benefit from a higher core count.

Final Thoughts

The CPU is one of the most critical components in any computer build, directly impacting the system's performance across all tasks. By understanding what the CPU does, the key differences between Intel and AMD processors, and how to choose the right one for your needs, you're well on your way to designing a system that fits your goals.

Next, we'll explore the **motherboard**, the component that connects and supports all your other parts, ensuring your CPU and other hardware work seamlessly together.

Chapter 5: The Motherboard

The motherboard is the backbone of your computer, connecting all components and ensuring they work together seamlessly. Choosing the right motherboard is critical for compatibility and performance, as it determines what parts you can use, how efficiently your system operates, and what features are available to you. In this chapter, we'll explore the role of the motherboard, the importance of compatibility, the different form factors, and the key features to consider when making your choice.

The Role of the Motherboard in a Computer Build

At its most basic level, the motherboard acts as the central hub for your PC. It is a printed circuit board (PCB) that allows the CPU, RAM, storage, GPU, and other components to communicate with each other. Think of it as the nervous system of your computer.

What the Motherboard Does

1. **Facilitates Communication:** The motherboard connects all components, allowing data to flow between the CPU, RAM, storage drives, and peripherals.

2. **Provides Power Distribution:** It distributes power from the PSU to the various components via dedicated connectors.
3. **Controls Features:** The motherboard's chipset controls features like overclocking, USB ports, and storage options.
4. **Determines Expandability:** It dictates how many additional components you can install, such as extra RAM, storage drives, or GPUs.

Compatibility: The Foundation of a Successful Build

Motherboard compatibility is one of the most important aspects of your build. Choosing a motherboard that supports your other components ensures your system runs smoothly.

1. CPU Compatibility

The first step in selecting a motherboard is ensuring it supports your chosen CPU. Each CPU requires a specific socket and chipset:

- **Socket Type:** This is the physical interface where the CPU connects to the motherboard. For example:
    - Intel CPUs typically use LGA sockets (e.g., LGA1700 for 12th and 13th Gen Intel processors).

- AMD Ryzen CPUs use AM4 or AM5 sockets.
- **Chipset:** The chipset determines the features and capabilities of the motherboard, such as overclocking support and PCIe lane availability. Higher-end chipsets (e.g., Intel Z790 or AMD X670) offer more advanced features.

2. RAM Compatibility

The motherboard dictates the type, speed, and capacity of RAM you can use:

- **Type:** Modern motherboards support DDR4 or DDR5 RAM, so ensure compatibility with your RAM sticks.
- **Speed:** Check the motherboard's supported RAM speeds; faster RAM requires a motherboard capable of handling higher frequencies.
- **Capacity:** The number of RAM slots on the motherboard determines how much memory you can install.

3. Storage Compatibility

Motherboards support different storage interfaces:

- SATA ports for traditional HDDs and SATA SSDs.
- M.2 slots for NVMe drives, offering faster data transfer speeds.

4. GPU Compatibility

Ensure the motherboard has enough PCIe slots to accommodate your GPU. For high-end GPUs, look for a PCIe 4.0 or PCIe 5.0 slot for maximum performance.

Understanding Form Factors

Motherboards come in different sizes, known as form factors, which determine their physical dimensions and compatibility with computer cases. Choosing the right form factor ensures your motherboard fits inside your case and provides the features you need.

1. ATX (Standard Form Factor)

- **Size:** 12 x 9.6 inches.
- **Features:** ATX motherboards offer the most expandability, with multiple PCIe slots, plenty of RAM slots, and extensive connectivity options.
- **Use Case:** Ideal for gaming and content creation builds, where expandability and performance are priorities.

2. Micro-ATX (Compact and Affordable)

- **Size:** 9.6 x 9.6 inches.
- **Features:** Micro-ATX boards are smaller but still provide a good balance of features, including multiple RAM slots and PCIe slots, though fewer than ATX.
- **Use Case:** Suitable for budget or mid-tier builds that don't require extensive expansion options.

3. Mini-ITX (Small and Portable)

- **Size:** 6.7 x 6.7 inches.
- **Features:** Mini-ITX motherboards are designed for compact builds and typically include only one PCIe slot and two RAM slots.
- **Use Case:** Perfect for small form-factor PCs where space is limited, such as media centers or portable gaming rigs.

Choosing the Right Form Factor

When selecting a form factor, consider:

- The size of your case.
- The number of components you plan to install.
- The need for portability versus expandability.

Features to Look For in a Motherboard

Once you've decided on the form factor and ensured compatibility, evaluate the motherboard's features to ensure it meets your needs.

1. Ports and Connectivity

The motherboard determines the number and type of ports available for connecting peripherals:

- **USB Ports:** Look for a mix of USB 3.0, USB-C, and USB 2.0 ports to support a variety of devices.
- **Audio Jacks:** High-quality audio outputs are essential for gamers and creators.
- **Ethernet and Wi-Fi:** Some motherboards include built-in Wi-Fi for wireless internet, while others rely on Ethernet for wired connections.

2. RAM Slots

The number of RAM slots affects your ability to upgrade memory:

- Most ATX boards have 4 slots, allowing for dual-channel configurations and future upgrades.
- Micro-ATX and Mini-ITX boards may have only 2 slots, limiting expandability.

3. Storage Options

Check for the number and type of storage connectors:

- Multiple SATA ports for HDDs and SSDs.
- M.2 slots for NVMe SSDs, offering faster storage performance.

4. PCIe Slots

PCIe (Peripheral Component Interconnect Express) slots are used for GPUs, sound cards, and other expansion cards. Look for:

- **Full-Length Slots:** For GPUs and other large add-ons.

- **PCIe Versions:** Newer versions like PCIe 4.0 and 5.0 provide faster data transfer rates.

5. Chipset Features

The chipset affects the motherboard's overall capabilities:

- **Overclocking Support:** Some chipsets, like Intel's Z-series or AMD's X-series, support CPU and RAM overclocking.
- **PCIe Lanes:** Determine the number of high-speed connections available for GPUs and storage drives.

Final Thoughts

The motherboard is the foundation of your computer build, influencing every component's compatibility and functionality. By understanding its role, choosing the right form factor, and evaluating its features, you can ensure your motherboard meets your needs and provides room for future upgrades.

In the next chapter, we'll delve into **RAM (Random Access Memory)**—an essential component that directly impacts your system's speed and multitasking capabilities.

Chapter 6: RAM (Random Access Memory)

When it comes to building a computer, RAM (Random Access Memory) plays a crucial role in determining how fast and efficiently your system operates. RAM is responsible for temporarily storing the data and instructions your CPU needs to perform tasks, acting as a high-speed bridge between your processor and long-term storage. In this chapter, we'll explore what RAM does, the differences in its speed, size, and DDR versions, and how to determine how much RAM is needed for various tasks.

What RAM Does and Why It Matters

RAM is a type of volatile memory, meaning it loses its stored data when the computer is powered off. Unlike your storage drives, which hold information permanently, RAM is designed for short-term data access. It provides the CPU with quick access to the information it needs to execute tasks without delay.

How RAM Works

Imagine you're working at a desk:

- Your **desk** is like your computer's RAM: it's where you keep the documents you're actively using, allowing you to work on them quickly.

- Your **filing cabinet** is like your computer's storage: it holds documents you're not currently using but want to keep for later.

When you open a program or file, the data is loaded from your storage drive into RAM so the CPU can access it quickly. The more RAM your computer has, the more data it can store for immediate use, leading to smoother multitasking and faster performance.

Why RAM Matters

1. **Performance:** Insufficient RAM can cause your computer to slow down, especially when running multiple applications or working with large files.
2. **Multitasking:** RAM allows you to switch between tasks without delays. For example, having more RAM makes it easier to stream videos, browse the web, and edit documents simultaneously.
3. **Gaming and Creative Work:** Modern games and creative software require significant amounts of RAM to load textures, process files, and maintain responsiveness.

Differences in Speed, Size, and DDR Versions

Not all RAM is created equal. Understanding the differences in speed, size, and DDR (Double Data Rate) versions can help you choose the best option for your build.

Speed

RAM speed, measured in megahertz (MHz), refers to how quickly it can transfer data to and from the CPU. Faster RAM can improve performance, especially in tasks that rely heavily on memory.

- **Standard Speeds:** Most modern systems use RAM with speeds ranging from 2400 MHz to 3600 MHz, though high-performance builds may use speeds exceeding 4000 MHz.
- **Latency:** Lower latency means faster response times. RAM labeled with "CL" (e.g., CL16) indicates the number of clock cycles it takes to complete a task. Lower CL values are better but often come at a higher cost.
- **Impact of Speed:** While higher RAM speed can boost performance, the improvement is most noticeable in memory-intensive tasks like video editing or gaming.

Size

The amount of RAM, measured in gigabytes (GB), determines how much data your system can handle at once. Larger amounts of RAM are essential for running multiple programs or working with large files.

- **Common Configurations:** Most builds use 8GB, 16GB, or 32GB of RAM.

- **Expandable Options:** Many motherboards allow you to add more RAM later, giving you flexibility for future upgrades.

DDR Versions

DDR versions indicate the generation of RAM technology, with newer versions offering faster speeds and better power efficiency. The most common versions are:

- **DDR3:** An older standard, mostly used in legacy systems. Speeds range from 800 MHz to 2133 MHz.
- **DDR4:** The current mainstream standard, offering speeds from 2133 MHz to 3600+ MHz. It's widely supported and cost-effective.
- **DDR5:** The newest generation, providing higher speeds and greater bandwidth. While it's more expensive and less widely supported, it's ideal for future-proofing high-end systems.

Your motherboard dictates which DDR version you can use. For example, a motherboard designed for DDR4 RAM cannot support DDR5 and vice versa.

How Much RAM Is Needed for Different Tasks

The amount of RAM you need depends on how you plan to use your computer. Below are recommendations based on common use cases:

Basic Office and Everyday Use

- **Recommended RAM:** 8GB
- **Why:** Tasks like web browsing, word processing, and video streaming don't require much memory. 8GB is sufficient for a smooth experience.

Gaming

- **Recommended RAM:** 16GB
- **Why:** Modern games demand more memory to load textures and handle background processes. 16GB ensures smooth gameplay and allows for multitasking (e.g., running Discord or streaming software alongside your game).

Content Creation and Professional Work

- **Recommended RAM:** 32GB or More
- **Why:** Applications like Adobe Premiere Pro, Blender, and large-scale CAD software require significant memory to process files, render videos, and manage complex projects. High RAM capacity ensures stability and responsiveness during intensive workloads.

General-Purpose Builds

- **Recommended RAM:** 16GB
- **Why:** A balanced amount of RAM allows for light gaming, multitasking, and casual media editing without performance bottlenecks.

Choosing RAM for Your Build

When selecting RAM, consider these factors:

1. **Compatibility:** Ensure the RAM you choose is compatible with your motherboard in terms of type (DDR4/DDR5), speed, and capacity.
2. **Dual-Channel Configuration:** For optimal performance, install RAM in pairs (e.g., two 8GB sticks for a total of 16GB) to enable dual-channel mode, which doubles data transfer speeds.
3. **Future Upgradability:** If you're on a tight budget, start with a lower capacity and ensure your motherboard has extra slots for expansion.

A Key Element of Your Build

RAM is an essential part of your computer, directly affecting its speed, responsiveness, and ability to handle demanding tasks. By understanding the differences in speed, size, and DDR versions, and by choosing the right capacity for your needs, you can ensure your system is ready to perform at its best.

As you move forward with your build, remember that RAM is one of the easiest components to upgrade, giving you flexibility to enhance your system in the future.

Chapter 7: Storage Options: HDD, SSD, and NVMe Drives

Storage is where all your computer's data—operating system, applications, files, and games—is saved. While it might seem simple, choosing the right storage solution can have a significant impact on your computer's speed, efficiency, and overall user experience. In this chapter, we'll explore the importance of storage speed and capacity, compare the three main types of drives—HDDs, SATA SSDs, and NVMe SSDs—and help you select the best storage options for your build.

The Importance of Storage Speed and Capacity

When it comes to storage, two key factors determine your computer's performance: speed and capacity.

Speed: The Gateway to Efficiency

Storage speed affects how quickly your computer can load programs, access files, and boot up. Faster drives significantly improve system responsiveness, reducing the time spent waiting for tasks to complete. Here's how speed impacts different scenarios:

- **Operating System Boot Time:** Faster drives enable your computer to start up in seconds rather than minutes.
- **Game Loading Times:** Modern games often require large amounts of data to load. Faster storage ensures smoother transitions between levels or environments.
- **File Transfers:** High-speed storage makes copying large files or accessing data-intensive applications seamless.

Capacity: Meeting Your Needs

Storage capacity refers to how much data your drive can hold, measured in gigabytes (GB) or terabytes (TB). Choosing the right capacity depends on your usage:

- **Light Users:** If you primarily browse the web, stream content, and use basic software, 500GB to 1TB is typically sufficient.
- **Gamers and Creators:** Games, videos, and creative projects require significantly more space. A combination of a fast SSD for primary tasks and a high-capacity HDD for bulk storage works well.
- **Data Hoarders:** If you store large amounts of data, such as extensive media libraries or backups, prioritize high-capacity drives like 4TB HDDs or larger.

Comparing HDDs, SATA SSDs, and NVMe SSDs

Each storage type has its strengths and weaknesses. Understanding these differences will help you choose the best option for your build.

HDD (Hard Disk Drive)

HDDs are the oldest and most cost-effective form of storage, relying on spinning magnetic disks to read and write data.

Advantages:

- **High Capacity at Low Cost:** HDDs offer large amounts of storage for a fraction of the cost of SSDs, making them ideal for storing massive files.
- **Reliable for Archiving:** HDDs are well-suited for long-term storage of infrequently accessed data.

Disadvantages:

- **Slower Speeds:** HDDs are significantly slower than SSDs, with read/write speeds typically ranging from 80 to 160 MB/s.
- **Mechanical Design:** The moving parts in HDDs make them more prone to physical damage and wear over time.
- **Longer Load Times:** HDDs take longer to boot up your operating system or load programs.

Best Use Case: Budget builds, bulk storage for media libraries, and data archiving.

SATA SSD (Solid-State Drive)

SATA SSDs are a major step up from HDDs, using flash memory to store data. They connect to the motherboard via SATA cables.

Advantages:

- **Faster Speeds:** SATA SSDs typically offer read/write speeds of 500–600 MB/s, significantly reducing boot times and program load times.
- **No Moving Parts:** SSDs are more durable than HDDs and less likely to fail due to physical shocks.
- **Affordable Performance:** While more expensive than HDDs, SATA SSDs provide excellent value for mainstream users.

Disadvantages:

- **Limited by SATA Interface:** While much faster than HDDs, SATA SSDs are slower than NVMe drives due to the constraints of the SATA connection.

Best Use Case: Primary drives for operating systems, frequently used programs, and casual gaming.

NVMe SSD (Non-Volatile Memory Express)

NVMe SSDs are the fastest storage option, using the PCIe interface instead of SATA. They are designed for speed and high-performance computing.

Advantages:

- **Blazing Speeds:** NVMe SSDs deliver read/write speeds of 3,500 MB/s or higher, making them ideal for data-intensive applications.
- **Efficient Multitasking:** Their advanced technology supports faster access to multiple files simultaneously.
- **Compact Design:** NVMe drives are small and fit directly into the motherboard's M.2 slot, saving space and reducing cable clutter.

Disadvantages:

- **Higher Cost:** NVMe drives are more expensive per GB compared to SATA SSDs and HDDs.
- **Overkill for Some Users:** The speed benefits may not be noticeable for light users or basic tasks.

Best Use Case: High-performance gaming, video editing, 3D rendering, and other demanding workloads.

Choosing the Right Drive for Your Build

The ideal storage setup depends on your needs, budget, and how you plan to use your computer. Here are some practical recommendations:

Budget Builds

For budget-conscious users, pairing a small SSD with a high-capacity HDD provides the best of both worlds:

- **SSD:** Use a 250GB or 500GB SATA SSD for the operating system and key applications.
- **HDD:** Add a 1TB or 2TB HDD for bulk storage, such as media files or backups.

Gaming Builds

Gamers benefit greatly from faster storage to reduce load times and improve overall responsiveness:

- **Primary Drive:** Use a 500GB NVMe SSD for the operating system and frequently played games.
- **Secondary Drive:** Add a 2TB HDD for less demanding games, media, and general storage.

Content Creation Builds

Content creators need fast storage to handle large files and improve workflow efficiency:

- **Primary Drive:** Opt for a 1TB NVMe SSD for the operating system, software, and active projects.
- **Backup Drive:** Include a 4TB HDD or external drive for long-term file storage and backups.

General-Purpose Builds

For users looking for a balance between performance and capacity:

- **SATA SSD:** A 1TB SATA SSD is sufficient for the operating system, applications, and casual storage needs.
- **Expandable Storage:** Choose a motherboard with extra M.2 slots or SATA ports for future upgrades.

Maximizing Your Storage Setup

- **Use Multiple Drives:** Combining different types of storage—like an NVMe SSD for speed and an HDD for capacity—gives you the best of both worlds.
- **Organize Your Data:** Keep your operating system and frequently accessed files on the fastest drive, while using slower drives for archives and backups.
- **Plan for Future Needs:** Ensure your motherboard has enough ports or slots to add more storage later if required.

The Building Blocks of Data

Storage is a critical component of your build, directly impacting your system's speed, capacity, and overall functionality. By understanding the differences between HDDs, SATA SSDs, and NVMe SSDs, you can choose the right combination to meet your needs and budget.

Keep your storage choices aligned with your goals, and you'll set yourself up for a system that runs smoothly, efficiently, and with plenty of room for growth.

Chapter 8: The GPU (Graphics Processing Unit)

The Graphics Processing Unit (GPU) is one of the most important components in modern computers, especially for tasks that involve rendering images, animations, and videos. Whether you're building a gaming rig, a content creation powerhouse, or a general-purpose PC, the GPU's performance can make or break your experience. In this chapter, we'll dive into what the GPU does, when you need a dedicated GPU, compare Nvidia and AMD GPUs, and provide guidance on selecting the best GPU for gaming, video editing, or 3D rendering.

What the GPU Does and When You Need a Dedicated One

The GPU is responsible for rendering images and graphics, transforming complex data into the visuals you see on your screen. While the CPU handles general-purpose computing, the GPU is designed for tasks that require massive parallel processing, such as:

- Rendering game environments and textures.
- Processing videos for editing or playback.
- Accelerating machine learning and AI workloads.

Integrated vs. Dedicated GPUs

GPUs come in two primary types: integrated and dedicated.

Integrated GPU

- **What It Is:** Built into the CPU, an integrated GPU shares system memory (RAM) to handle basic graphical tasks.
- **When It's Enough:**
    - Office work, web browsing, and light media consumption.
    - Casual gaming with minimal graphical demands.
- **Limitations:**
    - Limited performance for demanding tasks.
    - Can struggle with high-resolution displays or multiple monitors.

Dedicated GPU

- **What It Is:** A separate hardware component designed specifically for graphics processing, with its own memory (VRAM).
- **When You Need It:**
    - Gaming: To run modern games smoothly at high settings.
    - Video Editing: To process high-resolution footage and apply effects.
    - 3D Rendering: To handle the complex calculations required for creating detailed models and animations.

Nvidia vs. AMD GPUs

The GPU market is dominated by two major players: Nvidia and AMD. Both companies produce powerful GPUs, but they have distinct features, strengths, and ecosystems.

Nvidia GPUs

- **Strengths:**
  - Exceptional performance in ray tracing and AI-enhanced tasks, thanks to their proprietary RTX technology.
  - Advanced software features like DLSS (Deep Learning Super Sampling), which boosts performance by rendering images at lower resolutions and upscaling them with AI.
  - Broad driver support and compatibility with creative applications like Adobe Premiere Pro and Blender.
- **Popular Series:** GeForce RTX 3000 and 4000 series for gaming and creative tasks; Quadro cards for professional use.
- **Target Audience:** Gamers and professionals who want cutting-edge features and are willing to pay a premium.

AMD GPUs

- **Strengths:**
  - Competitive performance at lower price points, offering excellent value for money.

- ○ Radeon GPUs excel in high-resolution gaming, especially at 1440p and 4K.
- ○ Open-source technologies like FSR (FidelityFX Super Resolution) provide similar upscaling benefits as Nvidia's DLSS, without requiring proprietary hardware.
- **Popular Series:** Radeon RX 6000 and 7000 series for gaming and creative workloads.
- **Target Audience:** Budget-conscious gamers and creators looking for strong performance without overspending.

Which Is Better?

The choice between Nvidia and AMD depends on your priorities:

- **If You Want Cutting-Edge Features:** Nvidia's RTX series often leads in AI and ray tracing technology.
- **If You're Budget-Conscious:** AMD offers more affordable options with comparable performance in many cases.

How to Pick a GPU for Gaming, Video Editing, or 3D Rendering

The right GPU depends on your primary use case. Let's break down what to look for based on your specific needs.

1. Gaming

For gaming, the GPU is arguably the most critical component. It determines how well your system can render graphics, maintain high frame rates, and deliver smooth gameplay.

What to Look For:

- **VRAM:** Aim for at least 8GB of VRAM to handle modern games, especially at 1440p or 4K resolutions.
- **Ray Tracing:** If you want realistic lighting effects, choose a card that supports ray tracing, such as Nvidia's RTX or AMD's RX 6000/7000 series.
- **Refresh Rate Support:** Match your GPU to your monitor's refresh rate. For example:
    - A 1080p 144Hz monitor pairs well with a mid-range GPU like the Nvidia RTX 3060 or AMD RX 6700 XT.
    - A 4K 60Hz monitor benefits from a high-end card like the Nvidia RTX 4080 or AMD RX 7900 XTX.

Recommended GPUs:

- **Budget:** Nvidia RTX 3050, AMD RX 6600.
- **Mid-Range:** Nvidia RTX 3060 Ti, AMD RX 6700 XT.
- **High-End:** Nvidia RTX 4090, AMD RX 7900 XTX.

---

2. Video Editing

Video editing workloads require a GPU that can accelerate rendering, color grading, and encoding, especially when working with high-resolution footage.

What to Look For:

- **CUDA Cores or Stream Processors:** These cores handle the parallel processing needed for rendering and encoding. Nvidia GPUs with CUDA cores often integrate well with creative software like Adobe Premiere Pro.
- **VRAM:** High-resolution video (4K and above) benefits from GPUs with 8GB or more VRAM to handle larger frame sizes and effects.
- **Driver Support:** Choose a GPU with drivers optimized for creative applications.

Recommended GPUs:

- **Budget:** Nvidia GTX 1660 Super, AMD RX 6650 XT.
- **Mid-Range:** Nvidia RTX 3060, AMD RX 6800.
- **High-End:** Nvidia RTX 4080, AMD RX 7900 XT.

---

3. 3D Rendering and Animation

Rendering 3D models and animations involves complex calculations that demand powerful GPUs with high VRAM and processing capabilities.

What to Look For:

- **VRAM:** For 3D rendering, especially in applications like Blender, prioritize GPUs with at least 12GB of VRAM to handle detailed scenes.
- **Ray Tracing:** GPUs with ray tracing capabilities can accelerate rendering for realistic lighting and shadows.
- **Professional Cards:** If your work is strictly professional, consider workstation GPUs like Nvidia Quadro or AMD Radeon Pro cards for optimized drivers and certifications.

Recommended GPUs:

- **Budget:** Nvidia RTX 3060, AMD RX 6700 XT.
- **Mid-Range:** Nvidia RTX 3070, AMD RX 6800 XT.
- **High-End:** Nvidia RTX 4090, AMD RX 7900 XTX.

Balancing Performance and Budget

When selecting a GPU, consider these factors to strike the right balance:

1. **Resolution and Settings:** If you're gaming at 1080p, a mid-range GPU is sufficient, but 4K gaming or professional rendering demands high-end cards.
2. **Future-Proofing:** Invest in a GPU with more VRAM and newer technologies to ensure longevity.
3. **Power Supply Compatibility:** Ensure your PSU can handle the power requirements of your chosen GPU.

4. **Cooling and Size:** Check your case dimensions and airflow to ensure the GPU fits and stays cool under load.

Enhancing Your Build with the Right GPU

The GPU is the engine behind stunning visuals and fast rendering, making it a critical investment for gamers, creators, and professionals alike. Whether you're chasing high frame rates in the latest games, editing cinematic videos, or crafting intricate 3D designs, choosing the right GPU will ensure your system performs to its fullest potential. Take the time to evaluate your needs, research the latest offerings, and pick a card that aligns with your goals.

Chapter 9: The Power Supply Unit (PSU)

The Power Supply Unit (PSU) is one of the most critical yet often overlooked components in a computer build. Its job is to convert electricity from your wall outlet into usable power for your PC's components. A reliable PSU is essential not only for powering your system but also for ensuring stability, efficiency, and longevity. In this chapter, we'll discuss why a good PSU is crucial, how to calculate your power needs, and how to understand PSU ratings like 80 Plus Bronze, Gold, and beyond.

Why a Reliable PSU Is Crucial

A PSU is the heart of your computer's electrical system, distributing power to every component. Choosing a high-quality PSU ensures your system operates safely and efficiently. Here's why reliability matters:

1. Stability

A stable PSU delivers consistent power to your components, preventing voltage spikes or drops that could damage sensitive parts like the CPU, GPU, or motherboard. An unreliable PSU can lead to crashes, freezes, or complete system failure.

2. Safety

A poor-quality PSU increases the risk of overheating, short circuits, or even electrical fires. High-quality PSUs come with built-in protections, such as:

- Overvoltage Protection (OVP): Prevents excessive voltage from damaging components.
- Overcurrent Protection (OCP): Limits the current to safe levels.
- Short Circuit Protection (SCP): Shuts off the PSU in case of a short circuit.

3. Efficiency

Efficient PSUs waste less electricity as heat, which reduces energy costs and helps keep your system cooler. This is particularly important for high-performance PCs that consume more power.

4. Longevity

A reliable PSU not only lasts longer but also protects your components, extending the lifespan of your entire system. Investing in a good PSU saves money in the long run by avoiding costly repairs or replacements.

Calculating Your Power Needs

Before purchasing a PSU, it's essential to determine how much power your system will require. Overestimating can lead to unnecessary expenses, while underestimating may cause instability or even hardware damage.

1. Use a PSU Calculator

Online PSU calculators, such as those provided by **OuterVision** or **PCPartPicker**, are excellent tools for estimating your power needs. These calculators take into account:

- Your CPU and GPU models.
- The number of storage drives and other peripherals.
- Cooling solutions (e.g., fans, liquid coolers).
- Any planned overclocking.

2. Consider Peak Power Requirements

Components like GPUs and CPUs have peak power requirements during intensive tasks, such as gaming or rendering. A good rule of thumb is to add 20-30% to your calculated wattage for headroom, ensuring stability under heavy loads.

Example Calculation:

Let's say your system includes:

- An Intel Core i5 processor: ~125W.
- An Nvidia RTX 3060 GPU: ~170W.
- Two storage drives: ~20W.
- Case fans and peripherals: ~30W.

Your total estimated power requirement is 345W. Adding 30% headroom, you should choose a PSU rated for at least 450-500W.

3. Account for Future Upgrades

If you plan to upgrade components like your GPU or add more storage, select a PSU with enough capacity to handle these changes. For example, a system requiring 450W today may benefit from a 650W PSU to accommodate future upgrades.

Understanding PSU Ratings (80 Plus, Bronze, Gold)

PSUs are graded based on their energy efficiency using the **80 Plus Certification** system. This rating indicates how efficiently the PSU converts electricity from your wall outlet into usable power. The higher the rating, the less energy is wasted as heat.

The 80 Plus Ratings:

1. **80 Plus Standard:**
    - Efficiency: At least 80% efficiency at 20%, 50%, and 100% loads.
    - Entry-level certification for basic systems.
2. **80 Plus Bronze:**
    - Efficiency: ~82-85% efficiency depending on load.
    - A popular choice for budget and mid-range builds.
3. **80 Plus Silver:**

- Efficiency: ~85-88% efficiency depending on load.
- Less common, offering slightly better efficiency than Bronze.
4. **80 Plus Gold:**
   - Efficiency: ~87-90% efficiency depending on load.
   - A great balance of performance and cost for gaming and professional builds.
5. **80 Plus Platinum:**
   - Efficiency: ~89-92% efficiency depending on load.
   - Designed for high-performance builds with lower heat output and reduced energy costs.
6. **80 Plus Titanium:**
   - Efficiency: ~92-94% efficiency depending on load.
   - The highest level of efficiency, ideal for enterprise and enthusiast systems.

Why Efficiency Matters

- **Reduced Heat:** A more efficient PSU generates less heat, improving system cooling and reducing fan noise.
- **Lower Energy Costs:** High-efficiency PSUs consume less power, saving money on electricity bills over time.
- **Longevity:** Components in high-efficiency PSUs are often of better quality, leading to increased durability.

How to Choose the Right PSU

Now that you understand the basics of power requirements and efficiency, here are the steps to choose the perfect PSU for your build:

1. Match Wattage to Your Needs

Ensure the PSU provides enough power for your components with some headroom for future upgrades. For most builds:

- Budget/Office PC: 400-500W.
- Gaming PC: 600-750W.
- High-Performance PC: 750-1000W or more.

2. Prioritize Efficiency

Aim for at least an 80 Plus Bronze-rated PSU for basic builds, and consider Gold or higher for gaming and high-performance systems.

3. Check Compatibility

Ensure the PSU has the right connectors for your components:

- 24-pin ATX connector for the motherboard.
- 8-pin or 6+2-pin connectors for GPUs.
- SATA and Molex connectors for storage drives and peripherals.

4. Choose a Reputable Brand

Stick to trusted PSU brands known for quality and reliability, such as:

- Corsair
- EVGA
- Seasonic
- Cooler Master
- be quiet!

5. Consider Modular Cables

Modular PSUs allow you to attach only the cables you need, reducing clutter and improving airflow inside your case. They come in:

- **Fully Modular:** All cables are detachable.
- **Semi-Modular:** Some essential cables are fixed, while others are detachable.
- **Non-Modular:** All cables are permanently attached.

Investing in Stability and Longevity

The PSU is a vital component that powers your entire system, making it worth the investment. By calculating your power needs, choosing the right wattage, and understanding efficiency ratings, you can ensure your PC runs reliably, safely, and efficiently. A high-quality PSU not only protects your components but also contributes to a quieter and cooler system. Choose wisely, and your PSU will provide stable performance for years to come.

Chapter 10: The Case

The computer case may seem like a purely aesthetic choice, but it plays a critical role in your build. Beyond housing all your components, it affects airflow, cooling, cable management, and even ease of assembly. In this chapter, we'll explore how to choose the right case based on size, cooling, and aesthetics, introduce some popular case brands and features, and discuss how to optimize airflow and cable organization for a clean, efficient build.

Choosing a Case Based on Size, Cooling, and Aesthetics

When selecting a case, it's important to consider more than just looks. The size of your case dictates compatibility with components, while its design impacts cooling performance and usability.

1. Size: Matching Your Case to Your Build

Computer cases come in various sizes, typically corresponding to motherboard form factors. Choosing the right size ensures compatibility with your components and enough space for upgrades.

- **Full Tower:**
    - Fits: ATX, Micro-ATX, and Mini-ITX motherboards.

- ○ Best For: High-performance builds, liquid cooling setups, or multiple GPUs.
- ○ Features: Ample space for components, excellent airflow, and room for custom cooling loops.
- ○ Drawbacks: Large and heavy, requiring significant desk or floor space.
- **Mid Tower:**
    - ○ Fits: ATX, Micro-ATX, and Mini-ITX motherboards.
    - ○ Best For: Most builds, including gaming and content creation PCs.
    - ○ Features: Balance of size and expandability, with good airflow and compatibility.
    - ○ Drawbacks: Slightly limited space for complex setups compared to full towers.
- **Mini Tower:**
    - ○ Fits: Micro-ATX and Mini-ITX motherboards.
    - ○ Best For: Budget or compact builds.
    - ○ Features: Smaller footprint, lightweight, and often more affordable.
    - ○ Drawbacks: Limited space for cooling and expansion.
- **Small Form Factor (SFF):**
    - ○ Fits: Mini-ITX motherboards.
    - ○ Best For: Portable or minimalist PCs.
    - ○ Features: Compact design, ideal for tight spaces or media centers.
    - ○ Drawbacks: Challenging to build in, with restricted airflow and component compatibility.

2. Cooling: Ensuring Proper Temperature Management

Good cooling is essential to prevent components from overheating, especially in high-performance builds.

- **Airflow Design:** Look for cases with mesh front panels and strategically placed vents for better airflow. Avoid cases with solid front panels, as they can restrict intake air.
- **Fan Support:** Most cases include pre-installed fans but offer additional mounting points for upgrades. Common fan sizes include 120mm and 140mm.
- **Liquid Cooling Compatibility:** If you plan to use an all-in-one (AIO) liquid cooler or a custom loop, ensure the case has radiator mounts and enough clearance for the cooling system.

3. Aesthetics: Matching Form with Function

A case's aesthetics allow you to personalize your build. Consider these design elements:

- **Tempered Glass Panels:** Showcase your components with a clear side panel.
- **RGB Lighting:** Many cases come with RGB fans or strips to add a splash of color.
- **Cable Shrouds and Panels:** Keep your build looking clean by hiding cables behind panels or PSU shrouds.

Popular Case Brands and Features

Many manufacturers design high-quality cases that cater to different preferences and budgets. Here are some of the most popular brands and their standout features:

1. NZXT

- Known for minimalist designs and excellent cable management.
- Offers cases like the NZXT H510, which is beginner-friendly and sleek.
- Popular among gamers and content creators.

2. Corsair

- Provides a wide range of cases, from budget-friendly to high-end options.
- Cases like the Corsair 4000D emphasize airflow and build quality.
- Often include integrated RGB lighting and fan control.

3. Cooler Master

- Specializes in versatile cases with excellent cooling support.
- The Cooler Master MasterBox series offers great value for mid-tier builds.
- Ideal for users who prioritize airflow.

4. Lian Li

- Known for premium, aluminum-built cases with a focus on aesthetics.
- Cases like the Lian Li O11 Dynamic are favored for custom liquid cooling setups.
- Excellent for advanced builders looking for stylish, high-performance options.

5. Fractal Design

- Offers understated, professional-looking cases with a focus on noise reduction.
- The Define series provides sound-dampening panels and a clean interior layout.
- Great for office or workstation builds.

6. Phanteks

- Combines innovative designs with affordability.
- Cases like the Phanteks Eclipse series are spacious and feature-rich.
- Popular for gaming and creative builds.

Managing Airflow and Cable Organization

Efficient airflow and clean cable management improve both performance and aesthetics. Here's how to optimize each:

1. Managing Airflow

Proper airflow ensures that cool air reaches your components while hot air is expelled. Follow these tips:

- **Fan Placement:**
    - Intake fans should be positioned at the front or bottom of the case to pull in cool air.
    - Exhaust fans should be placed at the rear or top of the case to expel hot air.
- **Positive vs. Negative Pressure:**
    - **Positive Pressure:** More intake than exhaust fans; reduces dust buildup but may trap heat.
    - **Negative Pressure:** More exhaust than intake fans; better cooling but prone to dust entry.
- **Filters:** Look for cases with removable dust filters to keep your system clean and maintain airflow.

2. Cable Organization

Tidy cable management not only improves airflow but also enhances the visual appeal of your build.

Tips for Cable Management:

- **Use Cable Cutouts:** Route cables through designated cutouts in the case to keep them out of sight.
- **Velcro Straps and Zip Ties:** Secure cables to the case using reusable straps or zip ties.
- **PSU Shroud:** Cases with PSU shrouds hide unsightly cables from the power supply.

- **Plan Ahead:** Before installing components, consider how cables will be routed to minimize clutter.

The Case as Your Build's Foundation

The computer case is more than just a shell; it's the foundation that ties your entire build together. Choosing the right case ensures your components fit, stay cool, and look great. Whether you prioritize size, cooling, or aesthetics, there's a case to match your vision. Take your time selecting a model that fits your needs and allows for an efficient, enjoyable building experience.

Chapter 11: Cooling Systems

Keeping your computer cool is critical for maintaining performance, extending the life of your components, and ensuring stable operation. Cooling systems prevent components like the CPU and GPU from overheating during intensive tasks like gaming, video editing, or 3D rendering. In this chapter, we'll explore the differences between air and liquid cooling, how to choose the right CPU cooler, and how to set up case fans for optimal airflow.

Air Cooling vs. Liquid Cooling

There are two primary methods of cooling a computer: air cooling and liquid cooling. Each has its strengths and weaknesses, and the right choice depends on your specific needs, budget, and preferences.

1. Air Cooling

Air cooling uses fans and heatsinks to dissipate heat from your components.

How It Works:

- A heatsink, typically made of metal, absorbs heat from the component (e.g., the CPU).

- A fan attached to the heatsink blows air across its fins to disperse heat into the surrounding air.

Advantages:

- **Affordability:** Air coolers are generally less expensive than liquid cooling systems.
- **Simplicity:** They are easy to install and require minimal maintenance.
- **Reliability:** With no moving liquids, the risk of leaks or mechanical failure is low.

Disadvantages:

- **Noise Levels:** Larger fans can generate noticeable noise, especially under load.
- **Aesthetic Limitations:** Air coolers are often bulkier and less visually appealing than liquid coolers.

Best For: Budget-conscious builders and those prioritizing reliability and ease of use.

---

2. Liquid Cooling

Liquid cooling systems, also known as water cooling, use liquid to transfer heat away from components.

How It Works:

- A pump circulates coolant through a loop of tubes connected to a water block, which absorbs heat from the component.

- The liquid travels to a radiator, where fans cool it down before it recirculates.

Advantages:

- **Superior Cooling Performance:** Liquid cooling is more efficient at handling high heat loads, making it ideal for overclocked or high-performance systems.
- **Quiet Operation:** Liquid coolers often run quieter than air coolers because they don't rely solely on fans.
- **Aesthetic Appeal:** Many liquid cooling systems feature sleek designs and customizable RGB lighting.

Disadvantages:

- **Higher Cost:** Liquid coolers are more expensive than air coolers, especially custom loops.
- **Complex Installation:** Setting up a liquid cooling system can be challenging, especially for beginners.
- **Risk of Leaks:** While rare, leaks can damage your components.

Best For: High-performance builds, overclocking enthusiasts, and users seeking a clean, modern look.

Choosing a CPU Cooler: Stock vs. Aftermarket

The CPU cooler is one of the most important parts of your cooling system, as the CPU generates significant heat during operation. Your choice between a stock cooler and an aftermarket cooler depends on your performance needs.

Stock Coolers

- **What They Are:** Stock coolers are included with many CPUs, particularly budget and mid-range models. Examples include AMD's Wraith Spire and Intel's stock coolers.
- **Advantages:**
    - Free with your CPU.
    - Easy to install and sufficient for non-intensive tasks.
- **Disadvantages:**
    - Limited cooling performance, especially for gaming or overclocking.
    - Less efficient at handling heat under heavy loads, leading to higher noise levels.

Best For: Office builds, basic systems, or users not planning to overclock.

Aftermarket Coolers

- **What They Are:** Aftermarket coolers are sold separately and offer superior performance compared to stock coolers. They are available in both air and liquid cooling variants.
- **Advantages:**

- Better cooling efficiency, allowing for lower temperatures and quieter operation.
- Essential for overclocking, where additional cooling is required.
- Aesthetic options, including RGB lighting and sleeker designs.
- **Disadvantages:**
  - Higher cost.
  - Installation may be more complex than stock coolers.

Types of Aftermarket Coolers:

1. **Air Coolers:**
   - Large heatsinks paired with high-performance fans.
   - Examples: Noctua NH-D15, Cooler Master Hyper 212.
   - Ideal for reliable cooling at a moderate price point.
2. **All-in-One (AIO) Liquid Coolers:**
   - Preassembled liquid cooling systems with integrated pump, radiator, and tubes.
   - Examples: Corsair H100i, NZXT Kraken series.
   - Best for builders seeking efficient cooling with minimal maintenance.
3. **Custom Loop Liquid Coolers:**
   - Fully customizable liquid cooling systems for advanced users.
   - Ideal for enthusiasts who prioritize aesthetics and ultimate cooling performance.

Best For: Gamers, content creators, and those overclocking their CPU.

Case Fan Setups for Optimal Airflow

Good airflow is essential to keeping all your components cool. Proper case fan placement ensures a steady flow of air through your case, removing heat and maintaining system stability.

1. Understanding Airflow Dynamics

Airflow in a computer case is created by a combination of intake and exhaust fans:

- **Intake Fans:** Pull cool air into the case, typically located at the front or bottom.
- **Exhaust Fans:** Push hot air out of the case, usually positioned at the rear or top.

2. Positive vs. Negative Pressure

- **Positive Pressure:** More intake fans than exhaust fans.
    - Benefits: Reduces dust buildup as air is pushed out of the case.
    - Drawbacks: Can trap heat if airflow isn't well managed.
- **Negative Pressure:** More exhaust fans than intake fans.

- Benefits: Removes heat effectively.
- Drawbacks: More prone to dust entering the case.

3. Optimal Fan Placement

To ensure proper airflow, follow these guidelines:

- **Front Intake Fans:** Draw cool air into the case.
- **Rear and Top Exhaust Fans:** Remove hot air from the case.
- **Side Panel Fans:** Optional for additional airflow but can disrupt overall dynamics.

4. Fan Size and Speed

- **Fan Sizes:** Common sizes are 120mm and 140mm. Larger fans move more air with less noise.
- **Fan Speed:** Measured in RPM (rotations per minute). Adjustable-speed fans let you balance cooling and noise levels.

5. Dust Filters

Choose a case with removable dust filters on intake vents to prevent dust buildup. Clean these filters regularly to maintain airflow efficiency.

Keeping Your Build Cool and Efficient

A well-designed cooling system is critical for maintaining your PC's performance and longevity. Whether you choose air cooling or liquid cooling, invest in a solution that matches your system's demands. Combine your CPU cooler with an optimized fan setup, and you'll ensure that your PC runs cool, quiet, and stable, even under heavy loads.

Chapter 12: Peripherals: Monitors, Keyboards, and Mice

Peripherals like monitors, keyboards, and mice are your primary tools for interacting with your computer. They not only influence your productivity but also enhance your overall computing experience, whether you're gaming, working, or just browsing the web. In this chapter, we'll guide you through choosing peripherals that complement your build, provide an overview of monitor types, and highlight the differences between gaming and productivity-focused peripherals.

Choosing Peripherals to Match Your Build

Peripherals should align with the purpose of your build, balancing functionality, aesthetics, and budget. Here are some key factors to consider:

1. Purpose-Driven Selection

- **Gaming Builds:** Prioritize peripherals with features like high refresh rates, customizable RGB lighting, programmable keys, and ergonomic designs.
- **Content Creation and Productivity Builds:** Focus on accuracy, comfort, and multitasking

capabilities, such as color-accurate monitors, ergonomic keyboards, and precision mice.
- **General Use Builds:** Seek peripherals that provide a balance between comfort and performance without overspending.

2. Compatibility and Connectivity

Ensure your peripherals are compatible with your system and match your desired connectivity preferences:

- **Wired Peripherals:** Offer faster response times and don't rely on batteries, making them ideal for gaming or productivity setups.
- **Wireless Peripherals:** Provide a cleaner setup and greater flexibility, especially for office or general-purpose builds. Look for low-latency options for gaming.

3. Aesthetic Considerations

- RGB lighting is a popular choice for gaming setups, allowing for customizable colors and effects.
- Sleek, minimalist designs are often favored for productivity or professional builds.

Overview of Monitor Types

A monitor is one of the most important peripherals, as it directly impacts your visual experience. Choosing the right monitor involves understanding key specifications like refresh rates, resolution, and panel types.

1. Refresh Rates

The refresh rate, measured in Hertz (Hz), determines how many times the screen refreshes per second. A higher refresh rate results in smoother visuals:

- **60Hz:** Standard for basic office or casual use.
- **120Hz – 144Hz:** Ideal for gaming, offering smoother motion and reduced input lag.
- **240Hz or Higher:** Designed for competitive gaming, providing ultra-smooth visuals.

2. Resolution

Monitor resolution affects the sharpness and clarity of the display. Common resolutions include:

- **1080p (Full HD):** Affordable and suitable for most users, especially for monitors up to 24 inches.
- **1440p (Quad HD):** Offers a noticeable improvement in clarity and is perfect for gaming or productivity.
- **4K (Ultra HD):** Provides exceptional detail, ideal for content creation and high-end gaming. Requires a powerful GPU to handle smoothly.
- **Ultra-Wide:** These monitors expand horizontal screen space, enhancing multitasking and immersive gaming.

3. Panel Types

Monitor panels influence color accuracy, response times, and viewing angles. The three main types are:

- **TN (Twisted Nematic):**
    - Pros: Fast response times and high refresh rates, making them ideal for competitive gaming.
    - Cons: Limited color accuracy and narrow viewing angles.
- **IPS (In-Plane Switching):**
    - Pros: Superior color reproduction and wide viewing angles, excellent for content creation and general use.
    - Cons: Slower response times and higher cost compared to TN panels.
- **VA (Vertical Alignment):**
    - Pros: Deep contrast and better color accuracy than TN panels, great for media consumption.
    - Cons: Slower response times can lead to motion blur in fast-paced gaming.

Gaming vs. Productivity-Focused Peripherals

The right peripherals can significantly enhance your experience, but their priorities differ between gaming and productivity.

1. Keyboards

The keyboard is an essential input device, and its features should match your needs.

Gaming Keyboards:

- **Mechanical Switches:** Provide tactile feedback and faster response times. Common types include:
    - **Linear (e.g., Cherry MX Red):** Smooth and silent, ideal for fast-paced gaming.
    - **Tactile (e.g., Cherry MX Brown):** Offer a slight bump for feedback.
    - **Clicky (e.g., Cherry MX Blue):** Loud and satisfying for gamers who enjoy audible feedback.
- **Programmable Keys:** Allow customization for in-game shortcuts.
- **RGB Lighting:** Adds style and enhances visibility in dark environments.

Productivity Keyboards:

- **Low-Profile Designs:** Slim and comfortable, reducing wrist strain for long typing sessions.
- **Ergonomic Layouts:** Curved designs and wrist rests to improve typing posture.
- **Wireless Options:** Minimize desk clutter, perfect for professional setups.

---

2. Mice

A well-chosen mouse ensures precise input and comfort, whether you're gaming or working.

Gaming Mice:

- **DPI (Dots Per Inch):** Adjustable DPI settings for precise sensitivity control.
- **Customizable Buttons:** Useful for binding in-game commands.
- **Ergonomic Designs:** Tailored for extended gaming sessions.
- **RGB Lighting:** Adds flair and matches other gaming peripherals.

Productivity Mice:

- **Ergonomic Focus:** Contoured designs to reduce strain during prolonged use.
- **Multi-Device Connectivity:** Some mice can switch seamlessly between devices.
- **Precision:** High DPI and smooth tracking for detailed work like graphic design.

---

3. Monitors

The choice of monitor directly impacts the quality of your experience.

Gaming Monitors:

- **High Refresh Rates:** Essential for smooth gameplay and reduced input lag.
- **Low Response Times:** Minimizes motion blur for fast-paced games.
- **Adaptive Sync Technologies:**

- **G-Sync (Nvidia):** Prevents screen tearing when paired with Nvidia GPUs.
- **FreeSync (AMD):** Similar technology for AMD GPUs.

Productivity Monitors:

- **High Resolution:** Improves clarity for detailed tasks like photo editing or video production.
- **Color Accuracy:** Monitors with high color accuracy (e.g., AdobeRGB or sRGB coverage) are ideal for creative professionals.
- **Multi-Monitor Support:** Expands screen real estate for multitasking.

Creating the Perfect Setup

Peripherals are your connection to your computer, and choosing the right ones enhances every interaction. Whether you're gaming, working, or simply browsing, matching your peripherals to your build ensures comfort, efficiency, and enjoyment. Invest in quality peripherals that align with your needs, and you'll notice the difference in your daily experience.

Chapter 13: Operating Systems and Software

The operating system (OS) is the backbone of your computer, providing the interface between you and your hardware. Alongside the OS, the right software ensures your PC is fully functional and tailored to your needs. In this chapter, we'll compare the three major operating systems—Windows, Linux, and macOS—explain how to obtain and install an OS, and highlight essential software for a newly built PC.

Windows, Linux, or macOS?

Choosing the right operating system depends on your build's purpose, your familiarity with each OS, and your budget. Each has its strengths and weaknesses, and your choice will shape your overall experience.

1. Windows

Windows is the most popular operating system, widely used for gaming, productivity, and general computing.

Strengths:

- **Compatibility:** Windows supports the broadest range of software, games, and hardware.

- **Gaming Performance:** Optimized for gaming with robust support for DirectX, high refresh rates, and adaptive sync technologies.
- **Ease of Use:** A familiar interface and vast resources make it accessible for beginners.
- **Software Support:** Compatible with productivity tools like Microsoft Office, Adobe Creative Suite, and engineering software.

Weaknesses:

- **Cost:** Windows licenses can be expensive, ranging from $100–$200 for retail versions.
- **Bloatware:** Pre-installed apps can clutter the system, requiring cleanup.

Best For: Gamers, general users, and those requiring compatibility with a wide range of software.

---

2. Linux

Linux is an open-source OS favored by developers, tech enthusiasts, and those seeking customization and control.

Strengths:

- **Free to Use:** Most Linux distributions (distros) are completely free.
- **Customizability:** Highly flexible, allowing users to modify the interface and functionality.
- **Lightweight Options:** Distros like Ubuntu, Mint, or Fedora can run efficiently on older or low-power systems.

- **Security:** Linux is less prone to malware and viruses due to its open-source nature.

Weaknesses:

- **Steeper Learning Curve:** New users may find Linux intimidating, especially when troubleshooting or using command-line tools.
- **Limited Software:** Some proprietary software and games may not be compatible, though alternatives often exist.

Best For: Developers, tech-savvy users, and those seeking a free, secure, and customizable system.

---

3. macOS

macOS is Apple's proprietary operating system, known for its seamless integration with Apple hardware and software.

Strengths:

- **User-Friendly Interface:** Intuitive and consistent design with minimal learning curve.
- **Creative Workflows:** Excellent support for media creation software like Final Cut Pro and Logic Pro.
- **Optimized Performance:** Works seamlessly with Apple hardware for reliable and smooth operation.

Weaknesses:

- **Hardware Requirements:** macOS is designed exclusively for Apple hardware, so it's not an option

for custom-built PCs (unless you're creating a Hackintosh, which has legal and compatibility challenges).
- **Cost:** Apple devices are expensive, making macOS an inaccessible choice for budget builders.

Best For: Users with Apple devices or those focused on creative workflows.

How to Obtain and Install an Operating System

Installing an OS is a critical step in making your PC functional. Here's how to get started:

1. Obtaining the OS

- **Windows:**
    - Purchase a license directly from Microsoft or authorized retailers.
    - Download the **Windows Media Creation Tool** from Microsoft's website to create a bootable USB drive.
- **Linux:**
    - Visit the website of your chosen distro (e.g., Ubuntu, Fedora, or Mint) and download the ISO file.
    - Use software like **Rufus** to create a bootable USB drive.
- **macOS (Hackintosh):**

- Follow specialized guides to install macOS on non-Apple hardware (note: this requires advanced knowledge and may violate Apple's terms of use).

2. Installing the OS

The installation process is straightforward for most operating systems:

1. **Create a Bootable USB Drive:**
   - Use tools like **Rufus** (Windows/Linux) or **Etcher** to create a bootable USB from the OS installer.
   - Insert the USB drive into your PC and boot from it by selecting the USB drive in the BIOS or boot menu.
2. **Follow the Installation Steps:**
   - **Windows:**
     - Select your language, region, and keyboard layout.
     - Enter your license key or choose to activate later.
     - Select the drive where you want to install Windows and proceed with installation.
   - **Linux:**
     - Boot into the live environment (optional) to test the OS.

- Choose the installation option, partition your drives, and follow on-screen instructions.
    - **macOS (Hackintosh):**
        - Follow community guides for creating and configuring the installation media and bootloader.
3. **Install Drivers and Updates:**
    - After installation, ensure your hardware functions properly by installing the latest drivers from the manufacturer's website.

Essential Software for a New PC

Once your OS is installed, equipping your PC with essential software ensures it's ready for daily use. Here's a list of must-have applications:

1. System Utilities

- **Antivirus Software:** For Windows, install reliable antivirus software like **Windows Defender**, **Bitdefender**, or **Norton**. Linux and macOS typically have fewer threats but may benefit from lightweight security tools.
- **Backup Tools:** Use **Macrium Reflect** or cloud-based options like **Google Drive** to protect your data.
- **Monitoring Tools:** Programs like **HWMonitor** or **CoreTemp** help monitor system performance and temperatures.

2. Productivity Software

- **Office Suites:** Install tools like **Microsoft Office, Google Workspace,** or open-source alternatives like **LibreOffice.**
- **Web Browsers:** Popular options include **Google Chrome, Mozilla Firefox,** and **Microsoft Edge.**
- **Cloud Storage:** Services like **Dropbox, Google Drive,** or **OneDrive** ensure you have access to files across devices.

3. Creative Tools

- **Photo Editing: Adobe Photoshop, GIMP** (free alternative).
- **Video Editing: Adobe Premiere Pro, DaVinci Resolve.**
- **Audio Editing: Audacity, Logic Pro** (macOS).

4. Gaming and Entertainment

- **Game Launchers:** Install platforms like **Steam, Epic Games Store,** or **GOG Galaxy.**
- **Media Players:** Tools like **VLC Media Player** or **Plex** offer versatile media playback.
- **Streaming Services:** Download apps for platforms like **Spotify, Netflix,** or **Twitch.**

5. Utility and Optimization Tools

- **Compression Software:** Tools like **WinRAR** or **7-Zip** for handling compressed files.
- **Disk Cleanup Tools: CCleaner** (use cautiously) or built-in OS cleanup tools to maintain performance.

Your Operating System, Your Control

The operating system and software you choose define how you interact with your PC and what it can achieve. Whether you opt for the familiar interface of Windows, the flexibility of Linux, or the creative ecosystem of macOS, selecting and setting up your OS is a vital step in making your build complete. Pair it with essential software tailored to your needs, and you'll be ready to unlock the full potential of your new computer.

Chapter 14: Setting a Budget

Building a computer is as much about planning as it is about assembling parts. Setting a realistic budget and allocating it wisely across your components ensures you get the best performance for your money while meeting your specific needs. In this chapter, we'll cover how to allocate your budget, prioritize upgrades, and identify areas where you can save without compromising on quality.

Allocating Your Budget Across Components

When determining your budget, it's essential to prioritize components based on their impact on your system's performance and your intended use. A well-balanced build ensures no single component bottlenecks the system.

1. Identify Your Use Case

Your purpose for building the PC will heavily influence how you allocate your budget. Here's a general breakdown by use case:

- **Gaming:** Focus on the GPU and CPU, as games rely heavily on graphics and processing power.

- **Content Creation:** Prioritize the CPU, RAM, and storage for handling large files and multitasking.
- **Office and Everyday Use:** Budget-friendly CPUs and integrated GPUs are sufficient; allocate more for reliable storage.
- **General-Purpose:** A balanced approach ensures good performance across a variety of tasks.

2. Component Budget Allocation

Here's a recommended percentage breakdown for allocating your budget:

High-Performance Gaming Build

- **GPU:** 40–50%
- **CPU:** 20–25%
- **Motherboard:** 10–15%
- **RAM:** 10–15%
- **Storage:** 10–15%
- **PSU:** 5–10%
- **Case and Cooling:** 5–10%

Content Creation Build

- **CPU:** 30–40%
- **GPU:** 25–30%
- **RAM:** 15–20%
- **Storage:** 10–15%
- **Motherboard:** 10–15%
- **PSU:** 5–10%
- **Case and Cooling:** 5–10%

Office or Budget Build

- **CPU:** 25–30%
- **Storage:** 20–25%
- **Motherboard:** 15–20%
- **RAM:** 15–20%
- **PSU:** 5–10%
- **Case and Cooling:** 5–10%

Prioritizing Upgrades and Where to Spend

Your budget may not allow you to buy the best components in every category. Knowing where to spend more and where you can cut back is key to getting the most out of your investment.

1. Components to Prioritize

These parts have the most significant impact on performance and are worth allocating a larger portion of your budget:

GPU (Graphics Processing Unit)

- **Why It's Important:** The GPU is critical for gaming, 3D rendering, and video editing. A good GPU ensures smooth performance and better visuals.

- **When to Spend More:** If your build focuses on gaming or creative tasks, invest in a higher-end GPU to avoid bottlenecks.

CPU (Central Processing Unit)

- **Why It's Important:** The CPU handles all processing tasks. A powerful CPU ensures your system runs efficiently, especially for multitasking and content creation.
- **When to Spend More:** If you're editing videos, streaming, or running multiple demanding programs, prioritize a multi-core processor.

Motherboard

- **Why It's Important:** The motherboard connects all components, ensuring compatibility and performance.
- **When to Spend More:** If you need advanced features like overclocking support, PCIe 4.0/5.0, or extra connectivity, consider investing in a higher-end motherboard.

---

2. Components to Save On

These parts don't always require top-tier options and can be adjusted based on your budget:

RAM

- **When to Save:** 16GB of RAM is sufficient for most gaming and general-purpose builds. Only spend

more for content creation or multitasking-heavy workloads requiring 32GB or more.
- **Where to Look:** Budget-friendly brands often perform similarly to premium options as long as they meet speed and compatibility requirements.

Storage

- **When to Save:** Start with a modest-sized SSD (500GB or 1TB) and add more storage later. Pairing an SSD with a budget-friendly HDD for bulk storage can cut costs.
- **Where to Look:** SATA SSDs are cheaper than NVMe drives and still offer excellent performance for everyday tasks.

Case

- **When to Save:** Many budget cases offer good airflow and functionality. Aesthetic features like tempered glass and RGB lighting can often be skipped to save money.
- **Where to Look:** Focus on cases with good airflow and build quality, avoiding unnecessary extras.

Cooling

- **When to Save:** Stock coolers included with CPUs are sufficient for non-overclocked builds. Spend on aftermarket coolers only if you're overclocking or need better aesthetics and noise control.

PSU

- **When to Save:** Choose a reliable PSU with an 80 Plus Bronze rating or higher, but avoid overspending on unnecessary wattage.
- **Where to Look:** Stick to trusted brands with a good reputation for reliability, even for budget PSUs.

Tips for Maximizing Your Budget

1. Plan for Upgrades

If your budget is tight, consider starting with essential components and upgrading later:

- Install a single 8GB or 16GB RAM stick initially, then add more as needed.
- Use a smaller SSD for your operating system and expand storage later.

---

2. Consider Refurbished or Used Components

Buying refurbished or used components can save money without sacrificing quality. Stick to reliable marketplaces and verify warranties when purchasing second-hand parts.

---

3. Take Advantage of Sales

Watch for discounts during major sales events like Black Friday, Cyber Monday, or back-to-school sales. Online retailers like Amazon and Newegg often offer significant deals on components.

---

4. Build for Your Needs, Not Trends

It's easy to be tempted by the latest high-end components, but focus on what you actually need. Spending extra on features you won't use wastes money that could be better allocated elsewhere.

Smart Spending for a Balanced Build

Setting and sticking to a budget ensures you get the most out of your investment without overspending. By allocating funds strategically, prioritizing key components, and knowing where to save, you can build a system that meets your needs and leaves room for future upgrades. Whether you're a gamer, creator, or casual user, careful budgeting will help you build a PC you'll love while staying within your financial limits.

Chapter 15: Where to Buy Components

Choosing where to buy your PC components is just as important as selecting the right parts. A reliable retailer ensures quality, fair pricing, and customer support, while also protecting you from counterfeit or defective products. In this chapter, we'll cover the best websites and stores for purchasing components, tips for finding deals while avoiding scams, and considerations for buying used parts.

Reliable Websites and Stores

A variety of online and physical retailers cater to PC builders, each with unique benefits and drawbacks. Here are the most trusted options:

1. Newegg

- **Why It's Great:**
    - Specializes in PC components with a wide selection of parts, including GPUs, CPUs, motherboards, and peripherals.
    - Regular deals and discounts during major sales events.
    - User reviews for each product help you assess quality.

- **Watch Out For:** Third-party sellers on Newegg's marketplace, as they may not offer the same reliability as Newegg itself.

2. Amazon

- **Why It's Great:**
  - Massive inventory, including many PC components with fast shipping through Prime.
  - Competitive pricing, with frequent deals and discounts.
  - Reliable return policy if a product is defective.
- **Watch Out For:** Third-party sellers with less-than-stellar reviews. Always verify the seller before purchasing.

3. Micro Center

- **Why It's Great:**
  - Physical stores with knowledgeable staff who can offer advice and troubleshoot problems.
  - Excellent in-store deals, especially on CPUs and motherboard bundles.
  - A great option for same-day component purchases.
- **Watch Out For:** Limited store locations, as Micro Center isn't available in every region.

4. Best Buy

- **Why It's Great:**
    - Physical stores for hands-on shopping and convenient returns.
    - Good selection of mainstream PC components, including GPUs and SSDs.
    - Price matching for online competitors like Amazon or Newegg.
- **Watch Out For:** Limited selection compared to specialized PC retailers.

5. B&H Photo Video

- **Why It's Great:**
    - Trusted retailer with a solid reputation for PC components and electronics.
    - Competitive pricing and frequent sales.
    - Free shipping on many items.
- **Watch Out For:** Inventory may not be as extensive as Newegg or Amazon.

6. Local Computer Shops

- **Why It's Great:**
    - Personalized service and the ability to inspect parts before buying.

- Some shops offer used or refurbished components at reasonable prices.
- **Watch Out For:** Higher prices compared to online stores and limited stock.

Tips for Finding Deals and Avoiding Scams

Building a PC can get expensive, but with the right approach, you can find quality components at lower prices. Follow these tips to maximize savings and avoid pitfalls:

1. Use Price Tracking Tools

- Websites like **PCPartPicker** not only help you build a compatible system but also track prices across multiple retailers, notifying you of sales and price drops.
- Tools like **Honey** or **CamelCamelCamel** can monitor Amazon prices for discounts.

2. Look for Sales and Promotions

- Watch for major sales events like **Black Friday**, **Cyber Monday**, or **Prime Day** for significant discounts on components.

- Many retailers offer **bundle deals** (e.g., CPU + motherboard bundles) that save you money compared to buying items separately.

3. Compare Prices

Before purchasing, check multiple websites to ensure you're getting the best price. Many retailers offer price-matching policies, so don't hesitate to ask.

4. Avoid Counterfeit or Defective Products

- Stick to well-known retailers or authorized sellers. Avoid websites that seem too good to be true or don't have verifiable reviews.
- Check the packaging and product upon delivery for signs of tampering or damage.
- Verify warranties to ensure the product is genuine and protected by the manufacturer.

5. Be Cautious with Third-Party Sellers

When shopping on platforms like Amazon, eBay, or Newegg Marketplace:

- Check seller ratings and reviews.
- Avoid listings with vague descriptions or significantly lower-than-average prices.

- Ensure there's a return policy in case of defects or issues.

Considerations for Used Parts

Buying used or refurbished components can save you a lot of money, but it comes with risks. Here's how to shop safely for used parts:

1. Components to Consider Buying Used

- **GPUs:** Used GPUs can be a good deal, but verify their condition, as mining can put significant wear on the hardware.
- **CPUs:** CPUs are durable and generally safe to buy used, as long as there's no visible damage.
- **RAM:** Memory sticks are reliable and rarely fail, making them a safe bet for second-hand purchases.
- **Cases:** Computer cases are a low-risk purchase if in good condition.

2. Components to Avoid Buying Used

- **Storage Drives:** SSDs and HDDs degrade over time. Used drives may have reduced performance or fail sooner.

- **PSUs:** Power supplies are critical to system stability. Used PSUs may have wear that compromises reliability.
- **Motherboards:** Motherboards are fragile and difficult to diagnose for potential issues when buying used.

3. Where to Buy Used Components

- **eBay:** Offers a wide range of used parts, often with buyer protection. Look for sellers with high ratings.
- **Facebook Marketplace or Craigslist:** Local options allow you to inspect parts before purchasing, but exercise caution when meeting sellers.
- **Reddit Communities:** Subreddits like **r/hardwareswap** are excellent for finding used PC components, with a community-driven reputation system.

4. Questions to Ask Sellers

- Why are you selling the part?
- How old is the component, and has it been used intensively (e.g., for mining or overclocking)?
- Is the original packaging or receipt included?
- Does the part still have a valid warranty?

Smart Shopping for a Successful Build

Choosing the right retailer or marketplace for your PC components is crucial for ensuring quality, reliability, and a smooth building experience. Stick to reputable stores, compare prices, and use sales to your advantage. If you decide to explore the used market, take precautions to verify the condition and authenticity of parts. With the right strategy, you can build a powerful system while staying within your budget.

Chapter 16: Compatibility and Building Tools

Building a computer involves more than just buying the right components; ensuring compatibility between parts is critical for a successful assembly. Tools like **PCPartPicker** can simplify this process, but understanding the relationships between CPUs, motherboards, GPUs, and other components is equally important. Additionally, having the right physical tools and workspace can make assembly much smoother. In this chapter, we'll explore how to use PCPartPicker for planning, how to verify component compatibility, and which tools you'll need for assembly.

Using PCPartPicker to Plan Your Build

PCPartPicker is an invaluable tool for PC builders, offering a user-friendly platform to plan and optimize your build while avoiding compatibility issues.

1. What Is PCPartPicker?

PCPartPicker is an online tool that:

- Helps you select and organize components for your build.
- Checks for compatibility between parts.

- Tracks prices across multiple retailers to help you find the best deals.
- Provides a wattage estimate for your power supply needs.

2. How to Use PCPartPicker

Step 1: Create a Build

- Visit **pcpartpicker.com** and click on "**Start a System Build.**"
- Add components to your build by selecting categories like CPU, GPU, or motherboard.

Step 2: Check Compatibility

- PCPartPicker automatically flags any compatibility issues (e.g., mismatched CPU and motherboard sockets or insufficient power supply wattage).
- It also highlights warnings, such as potential clearance issues between large GPUs and compact cases.

Step 3: Budget and Optimize

- View real-time prices for your selected components from multiple retailers.
- Compare total build costs and adjust parts to fit your budget.

Step 4: Save and Share

- Save your build to revisit it later or share it with others for feedback and suggestions.

Understanding Compatibility Checks

Ensuring that all your components work together is a crucial part of building a PC. Below, we'll cover key compatibility considerations for CPUs, motherboards, GPUs, and other components.

1. CPU and Motherboard Compatibility

The CPU and motherboard must match in terms of:

- **Socket Type:** CPUs fit into specific sockets on the motherboard. For example:
    - Intel 12th and 13th Gen CPUs use the LGA 1700 socket.
    - AMD Ryzen 7000 Series CPUs use the AM5 socket.
- **Chipset:** The chipset determines motherboard features like overclocking support, PCIe versions, and connectivity. Higher-end chipsets (e.g., Intel Z790 or AMD X670) offer advanced capabilities.
- **BIOS Version:** Some motherboards may require a BIOS update to support newer CPUs.

2. RAM Compatibility

Motherboards dictate the type, speed, and capacity of RAM you can use:

- **DDR Type:** Check whether your motherboard supports DDR4 or DDR5 RAM.
- **Speed:** Ensure the motherboard supports your RAM's rated speed (e.g., 3200 MHz). Overclocking RAM may require enabling XMP (Intel) or DOCP (AMD) in the BIOS.
- **Capacity and Slots:** Verify the maximum RAM capacity and number of slots on your motherboard.

3. GPU and Motherboard Compatibility

GPUs connect to motherboards via PCIe slots, but there are additional considerations:

- **PCIe Version:** Modern GPUs are designed for PCIe 4.0 or 5.0, but they are backward-compatible with PCIe 3.0 slots.
- **Physical Clearance:** Ensure the GPU fits in your case and won't block other components.
- **Power Supply:** Check that your PSU provides sufficient wattage and the correct power connectors (e.g., 6-pin or 8-pin PCIe cables).

4. Case Compatibility

The case must accommodate all your components:

- **Motherboard Size:** Match your case to your motherboard's form factor (ATX, Micro-ATX, Mini-ITX).

- **GPU Clearance:** Ensure the case has enough space for the length and width of your GPU.
- **Cooling Support:** Check for radiator or fan mounting options if you're using liquid cooling.

5. Power Supply

Use tools like PCPartPicker's wattage calculator to ensure your PSU provides enough power. Add 20–30% headroom for future upgrades and peak loads.

Essential Tools for Assembly

Having the right tools and a suitable workspace is crucial for building a PC safely and efficiently. Here's a list of essentials:

1. Screwdrivers

- **Phillips #2 Screwdriver:** The most important tool for assembling a PC. Look for a magnetic tip to prevent losing screws.
- **Small Screwdriver Set:** Useful for M.2 drives and other tiny screws.

2. Anti-Static Equipment

- **Anti-Static Wrist Strap:** Grounds you to prevent electrostatic discharge (ESD), which can damage sensitive components.
- **Anti-Static Mat:** Provides a safe surface to assemble your PC.

3. Cable Management Tools

- **Zip Ties:** Secure cables for a clean and organized build.
- **Cable Clips or Velcro Straps:** Reusable alternatives to zip ties for bundling cables.
- **Wire Cutters or Scissors:** For trimming zip ties.

4. Tweezers

- Helpful for installing small screws or connecting delicate cables like front-panel headers.

5. Thermal Paste (Optional)

- If your CPU cooler doesn't come with pre-applied thermal paste, have a tube of high-quality paste like Arctic MX-4 or Noctua NT-H1 on hand.

6. Flashlight or Headlamp

- Provides better visibility in tight spaces, especially when working inside a case.

7. Cleaning Tools

- **Microfiber Cloths:** For wiping dust or fingerprints off components.
- **Compressed Air:** To clean dust from fans, heatsinks, or other components.

8. Additional Tools

- **Hex Driver or Wrench:** Sometimes needed for standoffs or case screws.
- **Plastic Spudger or Pry Tool:** Useful for handling delicate parts without scratching.

Preparing Your Workspace

Setting up a clean and organized workspace can make assembly easier:

- **Flat Surface:** Use a sturdy, non-conductive table or desk.
- **Good Lighting:** Ensure the area is well-lit to reduce mistakes.
- **Keep Components Organized:** Lay out all parts and tools before starting to minimize interruptions.

Building with Confidence

Using tools like PCPartPicker and understanding compatibility checks ensures your components will work together seamlessly. With the right physical tools and a prepared workspace, the assembly process becomes straightforward and enjoyable. Taking the time to plan and organize will save you frustration and lead to a successful build you can be proud of.

Chapter 17: Preparing Your Workspace

Building a computer requires a well-prepared workspace to ensure the process is smooth, efficient, and safe for both you and your components. A clutter-free, organized area helps minimize errors, while a static-free environment protects sensitive hardware. In this chapter, we'll cover how to set up a static-free workspace, organize your components and tools, and create an environment that makes assembling your PC an enjoyable experience.

Setting Up a Static-Free Environment

Electrostatic discharge (ESD) is one of the biggest risks to your PC components. Even a small static shock can damage sensitive hardware, so taking precautions is crucial.

1. Choose the Right Workspace

- **Flat and Stable Surface:** Use a sturdy, non-metallic surface like a wooden or plastic table. Avoid building your PC on carpeted floors or directly on metal surfaces.
- **Avoid Static-Prone Areas:** Carpeted rooms or environments with synthetic materials can generate

static electricity. If possible, build in a room with tile, wood, or concrete flooring.

2. Use Anti-Static Equipment

- **Anti-Static Wrist Strap:** Wear a wrist strap that grounds you to prevent static buildup. Clip the strap to a grounded metal object, such as your computer case or a power supply plugged into a grounded outlet (but turned off).
- **Anti-Static Mat:** Place an anti-static mat on your workspace and ground it using its attached clip. This provides a safe area to assemble components.
- **Ground Yourself Regularly:** If you don't have anti-static tools, touch a grounded metal object (like your unplugged case) frequently to discharge static buildup.

3. Avoid Creating Static

- **Wear Natural Fabrics:** Opt for cotton clothing instead of synthetic materials like polyester, which generate static.
- **Keep Humidity in Check:** Dry air increases static buildup. If possible, use a humidifier to maintain a humidity level of around 40–50%.

Organizing Your Components and Tools

An organized workspace not only makes the build process more efficient but also reduces the chance of losing small parts or making mistakes.

1. Lay Out Your Components

- **Keep Components in Their Boxes:** Until you're ready to install a part, leave it in its packaging to avoid accidental damage.
- **Group Similar Items:** Place related components (e.g., CPU, cooler, and thermal paste) together to streamline the assembly process.
- **Use Trays or Containers:** Use small containers or trays to hold screws, standoffs, and other tiny parts.

2. Arrange Your Tools

- **Essential Tools Nearby:** Keep tools like screwdrivers, tweezers, and zip ties within easy reach.
- **Organize Cable Management Supplies:** Place zip ties, Velcro straps, and wire cutters in a designated spot to simplify cable management later.
- **Avoid Clutter:** Keep unnecessary items off your workspace to maintain focus and avoid accidents.

3. Use a Checklist

Before starting the build, ensure you have all components and tools by creating a checklist. This prevents interruptions caused by missing items:

- **Checklist Example:**
    - CPU and cooler (with thermal paste if needed)
    - Motherboard
    - RAM
    - Storage drives
    - GPU
    - Power supply
    - Case
    - Screwdrivers, anti-static tools, zip ties, and cable management accessories

Preparing the Case

Before installing components, prepare your case to make assembly easier:

- **Remove Panels:** Take off the side panels of your case to access the interior. Store the panels in a safe place to avoid scratching them.
- **Check for Accessories:** Locate the accessory box inside your case, which contains screws, standoffs, and zip ties.

- **Install Standoffs:** Ensure motherboard standoffs are in place and align with your motherboard's mounting holes.

Create a Comfortable Environment

Your workspace should be as comfortable as it is functional. Building a PC can take a few hours, so setting up a conducive environment will make the process more enjoyable.

1. Lighting

- **Bright and Even Lighting:** Use overhead lights, desk lamps, or even a headlamp to illuminate your workspace and reduce the risk of mistakes.

2. Seating

- **Ergonomic Chair:** Use a comfortable chair to avoid strain during long assembly sessions. If standing, make sure the table height is comfortable to work at.

3. Minimize Distractions

- **Quiet Environment:** Avoid interruptions by choosing a quiet workspace. If you prefer

background noise, consider soft music or podcasts to keep you focused.
- **Phone on Silent:** Minimize distractions by silencing your phone or keeping it out of reach.

The Perfect Workspace for a Stress-Free Build

A well-prepared workspace is the foundation of a smooth and enjoyable PC building experience. By creating a static-free environment, organizing your components and tools, and setting up a comfortable area, you'll ensure that the assembly process is efficient and safe. Taking the time to prepare your space properly will save you from unnecessary frustration and let you focus on the excitement of building your custom computer.

Chapter 18: Step-by-Step Assembly

Building a computer can seem intimidating, but following a step-by-step approach ensures a smooth and efficient process. In this chapter, we'll guide you through assembling your PC, including installing the CPU and cooler, mounting the motherboard, inserting RAM and storage drives, and connecting the power supply and GPU. With patience and attention to detail, you'll have a fully functional system in no time.

Step 1: Installing the CPU and Cooler

The CPU and cooler are among the first components to install, as they require easy access to the motherboard.

Installing the CPU

1. **Prepare the Motherboard:**
    - Place the motherboard on a flat, static-free surface like an anti-static mat or its cardboard box.
2. **Open the CPU Socket:**
    - Release the socket retention arm by lifting it gently. This exposes the CPU socket.
3. **Align the CPU:**

- Match the gold triangle on the corner of the CPU with the corresponding marker on the socket.
- Carefully place the CPU into the socket without forcing it.
4. **Secure the CPU:**
   - Lower the retention arm to lock the CPU into place.

Installing the CPU Cooler

1. **Apply Thermal Paste (if needed):**
   - If your cooler doesn't have pre-applied thermal paste, apply a pea-sized amount to the center of the CPU.
2. **Attach the Cooler:**
   - Follow the cooler's instructions to align it with the mounting brackets on the motherboard.
   - Secure the cooler using screws or clips, ensuring it's firmly in place but not overtightened.
3. **Connect the Cooler Fan:**
   - Plug the cooler's fan cable into the CPU fan header on the motherboard, labeled "CPU_FAN."

Step 2: Mounting the Motherboard in the Case

Installing the motherboard requires care to ensure all connections align properly.

1. **Prepare the Case:**
    - Remove the side panels and locate the standoff screws inside the case.
    - Ensure the standoffs are installed in positions that match the holes on your motherboard.
2. **Install the I/O Shield:**
    - Snap the I/O shield (included with your motherboard) into the case's rear panel. Ensure it's aligned correctly with the motherboard ports.
3. **Position the Motherboard:**
    - Carefully place the motherboard into the case, aligning the mounting holes with the standoffs.
4. **Secure the Motherboard:**
    - Use screws from your case's accessory kit to secure the motherboard. Tighten the screws evenly, but avoid overtightening.

Step 3: Inserting RAM and Storage Drives

Adding RAM and storage drives is straightforward but requires precision to avoid damage.

Installing RAM

1. **Open the DIMM Slots:**
   - Push back the clips on the RAM slots.
2. **Insert the RAM Sticks:**
   - Align the notch on the RAM stick with the slot. It will only fit one way.
   - Push down firmly until the clips snap into place on both sides.
3. **Double-Check Placement:**
   - If you're installing two sticks, consult the motherboard manual to ensure they're placed in the correct slots for dual-channel mode (usually slots 1 and 3 or 2 and 4).

Installing Storage Drives

1. **2.5-Inch SATA SSDs or HDDs:**
   - Attach the drive to the case's drive bay using screws or a tool-free mounting mechanism.
   - Connect a SATA cable from the drive to the motherboard and a power cable from the PSU.
2. **M.2 SSDs:**
   - Locate the M.2 slot on the motherboard.

- Insert the M.2 drive at a slight angle and secure it with a screw provided by the motherboard.
3. **Double-Check Connections:**
    - Ensure all storage drives are firmly connected and secure.

Step 4: Connecting the Power Supply and GPU

Connecting the power supply and installing the GPU are the final steps to bring your system together.

Installing the Power Supply

1. **Position the PSU:**
    - Place the PSU in the designated compartment in the case, usually at the bottom.
    - Secure it with screws provided in the case's accessory kit.
2. **Connect Power Cables:**
    - **24-Pin ATX Cable:** Connect the large 24-pin cable to the motherboard's power connector.
    - **8-Pin CPU Cable:** Plug the 8-pin (or 4+4-pin) cable into the CPU power connector near the top of the motherboard.
    - **SATA Power Cables:** Connect these to your storage drives.

- **PCIe Cables:** Ensure you have enough PCIe cables for your GPU.

Installing the GPU

1. **Prepare the PCIe Slot:**
   - Remove the slot covers on the case that align with the PCIe slot on the motherboard.
   - Open the clip on the PCIe slot.
2. **Insert the GPU:**
   - Align the GPU with the PCIe slot and push it down firmly until the clip locks in place.
3. **Secure the GPU:**
   - Use screws from the case accessory kit to secure the GPU's bracket to the case.
4. **Connect PCIe Power Cables:**
   - Plug the PCIe power cables from the PSU into the GPU's power connectors.

Double-Check Your Work

Before powering on your system, review each component and connection:

- Ensure all screws are tightened but not overtightened.
- Verify all cables are securely connected.
- Check that fans, including CPU and case fans, are plugged into the correct headers.

A Complete System

Following these steps, your PC should now be fully assembled and ready for its first power-up. Building a computer is a rewarding experience, and by taking your time and double-checking each step, you've created a system tailored to your needs. Next, you'll install the operating system and configure your software to bring your build to life.

Chapter 19: Cable Management

Cable management is an essential part of building a clean and efficient PC. Properly organizing cables improves airflow, enhances cooling performance, and creates a visually appealing setup. In this chapter, we'll cover how to keep your cables organized for optimal airflow and share practical tips for using zip ties, Velcro straps, and other tools to achieve a tidy build.

Why Cable Management Matters

Organized cables do more than just make your PC look good—they also contribute to better performance and easier maintenance.

1. Improved Airflow

Messy cables can obstruct airflow, leading to higher temperatures for your components. Neatly routed cables keep air moving freely through the case, allowing fans and cooling systems to work efficiently.

2. Easier Maintenance

With tidy cables, accessing components for upgrades or troubleshooting becomes much easier. You won't need to untangle wires to swap out a GPU or add storage.

3. Aesthetics

A well-managed build looks professional and visually appealing, especially in cases with tempered glass panels that showcase the interior.

How to Keep Cables Organized for Better Airflow

Managing cables effectively starts with planning and using the right techniques.

1. Plan Your Cable Routes

Before connecting your components, map out where each cable will go:

- **Use Cable Cutouts:** Many cases have pre-designed cutouts to route cables behind the motherboard tray.
- **Follow Pre-Defined Paths:** Route cables along the edges of the case or behind panels to keep them out of sight and out of airflow paths.

2. Connect Components Strategically

- **Start with the PSU:** Plug in the power cables first and route them through the case. This helps you identify which cables will be visible and which can be tucked away.
- **Work from Back to Front:** Route cables behind the motherboard tray and bring them through cutouts to their connection points. This minimizes cable clutter in the main chamber.
- **Leave Slack for Adjustments:** Avoid pulling cables too tight. Leave a bit of slack to allow for easy adjustments during installation.

---

3. Group Similar Cables

Organize cables into groups based on their destination:

- **Power Cables:** Group all PSU cables together, such as the 24-pin ATX, 8-pin CPU, and PCIe cables.
- **Data Cables:** Bundle SATA and fan cables separately.
- **Front Panel Cables:** Keep small connectors for the front panel (power button, USB ports, audio) together.

Tips for Using Zip Ties and Velcro Straps

Zip ties and Velcro straps are invaluable tools for keeping cables tidy. Here's how to use them effectively:

1. Zip Ties

Zip ties are great for bundling cables into tight groups and securing them to the case.

How to Use Zip Ties:

1. **Bundle Cables:** Group cables that run in the same direction and secure them with a zip tie.
2. **Anchor to the Case:** Use built-in cable tie loops or anchor points on the case to secure cables in place.
3. **Trim Excess:** Cut off the excess length of the zip tie with wire cutters or scissors to prevent sharp edges.

Tips:

- Avoid overtightening zip ties, as this can damage cables or make future adjustments difficult.
- Use reusable zip ties for flexibility during future upgrades or maintenance.

---

2. Velcro Straps

Velcro straps are reusable and less restrictive than zip ties, making them ideal for managing bulkier cables or setups that require frequent adjustments.

How to Use Velcro Straps:

1. **Bundle Cables:** Wrap the strap around groups of cables and secure it snugly.
2. **Reposition as Needed:** Adjust Velcro straps easily without cutting or replacing them.

Tips:

- Use Velcro straps for areas where cables may need to be disconnected or rearranged, such as power cables connected to the PSU.

Tools and Accessories for Cable Management

In addition to zip ties and Velcro straps, several tools and accessories can help you achieve a professional-looking build:

1. Cable Clips and Anchors

- Stick-on cable clips or anchors can hold cables in place along flat surfaces.
- These are especially useful for routing cables in clean lines along the case edges.

2. Cable Sleeves

- Sleeves can group multiple cables together into a single, tidy bundle.

- Look for braided or fabric sleeves for a premium look.

3. Rubber Grommets

- Cases with rubber grommets around cable cutouts provide a cleaner appearance and prevent cables from rubbing against sharp edges.

4. Cable Shrouds

- Many modern cases come with built-in PSU shrouds to hide unsightly power cables.
- Use this area to tuck away extra cable length.

Final Touches for a Clean Build

Once you've routed and secured your cables, do a final check to ensure everything is in place:

- **Double-Check Connections:** Ensure all cables are plugged in securely, especially the 24-pin ATX, CPU, and GPU power cables.
- **Tidy Loose Ends:** Use extra zip ties or Velcro straps to secure any dangling cables.
- **Test Cable Tension:** Make sure cables aren't overly tight, which could strain connectors or components.

Effort Pays Off

Cable management is as much about functionality as it is about aesthetics. Taking the time to organize your cables improves airflow, simplifies maintenance, and elevates the overall look of your build. With proper planning and the right tools, you can achieve a clean, professional finish that showcases your hard work and makes your PC a joy to use.

Chapter 20: First Boot and BIOS Setup

After assembling your PC, the first boot is a moment of excitement and anticipation. This critical step verifies that all components are installed correctly and functioning properly. The BIOS (Basic Input/Output System) is the interface that helps you check your hardware's status, configure settings, and update firmware if needed. In this chapter, we'll guide you through checking for a successful boot, navigating the BIOS to confirm hardware recognition, and updating the BIOS for better stability.

First Boot: Checking for a Successful Boot-Up

The first time you power on your PC is when you'll determine if everything is functioning correctly. Follow these steps to ensure a smooth first boot:

1. Double-Check Connections

Before powering on your PC, review all connections:

- Verify that the 24-pin ATX and 8-pin CPU power cables are securely connected.
- Ensure the GPU's PCIe power cables are plugged in.

- Confirm that the front-panel connectors (power button, reset button, etc.) are attached correctly.
- Check that all fans, including the CPU and case fans, are connected to their appropriate headers.

2. Connect Peripherals

- Plug in a monitor, keyboard, and mouse. Use the GPU's display output if you've installed a dedicated GPU.
- Connect the power cable to the PSU and flip the PSU switch to "on."

3. Power On Your System

Press the power button on your case. Here's what to watch for:

- **Signs of a Successful Boot:**
    - Fans start spinning.
    - LEDs on the motherboard or case light up.
    - The monitor displays the motherboard's splash screen or BIOS interface.
- **If the System Doesn't Power On:**
    - Check the PSU switch and power cable.
    - Reseat the 24-pin and 8-pin power cables.
    - Verify the power button connector is properly attached to the motherboard.

4. Listen for Beep Codes or Error LEDs

If your system doesn't boot and your motherboard has a built-in speaker or debug LEDs, use these to identify the issue:

- Refer to the motherboard manual to interpret beep codes or LED indicators for hardware problems (e.g., RAM not seated correctly or GPU not detected).

Navigating the BIOS to Check Hardware Recognition

Once your system powers on successfully, you'll be greeted by the BIOS interface. The BIOS allows you to verify that all components are recognized and configure basic settings.

1. Accessing the BIOS

- Press the key indicated during boot (commonly **Delete**, **F2**, or **F10**) to enter the BIOS.

2. Confirming Hardware Recognition

In the BIOS, check that your hardware is properly detected:

- **CPU:** Look for the CPU model and clock speed under system information.
- **RAM:** Verify the total memory and speed. Ensure all installed sticks are recognized.
- **Storage Drives:** Confirm that all storage drives (HDD, SSD, M.2) are listed under the storage or SATA configuration menu.
- **GPU:** If your motherboard has a GPU detection section, ensure the dedicated GPU is listed.

3. Adjusting Key Settings

- **Set Boot Priority:** Under the boot menu, set your primary storage device (with the operating system installer) as the first boot option.
- **Enable XMP/DOCP for RAM:** If your RAM supports higher speeds, enable the XMP (Intel) or DOCP (AMD) profile in the memory settings to run it at its advertised speed.
- **Fan Profiles:** Configure fan speeds for optimal cooling in the hardware monitoring section.

Updating the BIOS for Better Stability

Updating your BIOS ensures compatibility with newer components and can improve system stability.

1. Determine If an Update Is Needed

- Check your motherboard manufacturer's website for the latest BIOS version.
- Compare the version listed on the website with the version displayed in your BIOS.

2. Download the BIOS Update

- Visit your motherboard manufacturer's support page and download the latest BIOS file for your specific model.
- Extract the file onto a USB flash drive formatted as FAT32.

3. Flash the BIOS

- Insert the USB drive into your PC and restart into the BIOS.
- Look for an option like **Q-Flash**, **EZ Flash**, or **M-Flash**, depending on your motherboard.
- Follow the prompts to select the BIOS file from the USB drive and initiate the update.

4. Let the Update Complete

- Do not power off your system or remove the USB drive during the update process. Your PC will reboot automatically when the update is finished.

Troubleshooting First Boot Issues

If your system doesn't boot or doesn't display the BIOS, here are common issues and fixes:

- **No Display Output:** Verify the monitor is connected to the GPU (not the motherboard, unless you're using integrated graphics).
- **Beep Codes or LED Errors:** Reseat the component indicated by the error (e.g., RAM or GPU).
- **Power Issues:** Check the PSU connections and ensure the PSU switch is set to "on."

The Foundation of Your Build

Successfully powering on your PC and configuring the BIOS is a major milestone in your build process. By verifying hardware recognition and updating the BIOS, you ensure that your system is stable and ready for the next step: installing the operating system and software. Take your time, double-check each connection, and enjoy seeing your hard work come to life!

Chapter 21: Installing Your Operating System

The final step in building your PC is installing an operating system (OS). This process turns your hardware into a functional computer. In this chapter, we'll cover how to boot from a USB drive, provide a step-by-step guide to installing either Windows or Linux, and explain how to set up drivers for optimal performance.

How to Boot from a USB Drive

Before installing the OS, you'll need to prepare a bootable USB drive and set your PC to boot from it.

1. **Create a Bootable USB Drive**

    - **Windows:**
        - Download the **Windows Media Creation Tool** from Microsoft's website.
        - Use the tool to create a bootable USB drive (at least 8GB) with the Windows installer.
    - **Linux:**
        - Download the ISO file for your chosen Linux distribution (e.g., Ubuntu, Fedora, Mint) from its official website.
        - Use software like **Rufus** (Windows) or **Etcher** (Linux/Mac) to create a bootable USB.

2. Set Boot Priority in BIOS

1. **Insert the USB Drive:**
   - Plug the bootable USB drive into your PC.
2. **Enter BIOS:**
   - Restart your PC and press the BIOS key (e.g., **Delete**, **F2**, or **F10**) during boot.
3. **Change Boot Order:**
   - Navigate to the boot menu and set the USB drive as the first boot option.
4. **Save and Exit:**
   - Save your changes and exit the BIOS. Your PC will restart and boot from the USB drive.

Step-by-Step Guide to Installing Windows

Windows is one of the most popular operating systems for gaming, productivity, and general use. Here's how to install it:

1. Start the Installation

- After booting from the USB drive, you'll see the Windows Setup screen.
- Select your language, time, and keyboard preferences, then click **Next** and **Install Now**.

2. Enter the Product Key

- If you have a product key, enter it. If not, click **I don't have a product key** to proceed. You can activate Windows later.

3. Choose the Edition

- Select the edition of Windows that matches your product key (e.g., Home, Pro).

4. Select Installation Type

- Choose **Custom: Install Windows Only** for a clean installation.

5. Partition the Drive

- Select the drive where you want to install Windows. If the drive is unallocated, click **New** to create a partition. Windows will format the drive and set it up for installation.

6. Complete Installation

- Windows will copy files and restart your PC several times during the installation. Follow the on-screen prompts to set up your account, connect to Wi-Fi, and configure privacy settings.

Step-by-Step Guide to Installing Linux

Linux is a versatile OS known for its customization and efficiency. Here's how to install it:

1. Start the Installation

- After booting from the USB drive, you'll see a live environment or installation menu.
- Select **Install [Distribution Name]** (e.g., Install Ubuntu).

2. Select Preferences

- Choose your language, keyboard layout, and installation type (e.g., Minimal Installation for basic apps or Full Installation for a complete setup).

3. Partition the Drive

- Select **Erase Disk and Install [Distribution]** to automatically partition the drive.

- For advanced users, choose **Something Else** to create custom partitions.

4. Configure Your Account

- Enter your name, username, and password. This account will have administrative privileges.

5. Complete Installation

- Linux will copy files and configure the system. Once done, restart your PC and remove the USB drive when prompted.

Setting Up Drivers for Optimal Performance

After installing the OS, you need to install drivers to ensure your hardware works at its best. Drivers are software that allows the OS to communicate with your components.

1. Install Motherboard Drivers

- Use the CD or USB drive provided with your motherboard, or download the latest drivers from the manufacturer's website.
- Install drivers for:
  - **Chipset:** Enables communication between the CPU and motherboard.
  - **Audio:** Ensures proper functioning of onboard audio.
  - **LAN/Wi-Fi:** Activates internet connectivity.

2. Install GPU Drivers

- Download the latest drivers from your GPU manufacturer's website:
  - **Nvidia:** Use **GeForce Experience** to download and install drivers.
  - **AMD:** Download drivers from the AMD Radeon Software page.
- Avoid using generic drivers installed by the OS, as they may not provide optimal performance.

3. Update Other Drivers

- **Peripherals:** Install drivers for keyboards, mice, and other peripherals if required.
- **Monitors:** Download color profiles or drivers for specialized monitors.

4. Use Windows Update or Linux Package Manager

- For Windows, run **Windows Update** to install additional drivers automatically.
- For Linux, use the distribution's package manager (e.g., APT for Ubuntu) to check for updates and install proprietary drivers if needed.

Testing Your System

Once drivers are installed, verify that everything is working:

- **Check Device Manager (Windows):** Ensure all devices are listed without errors.
- **Run Benchmark Tests:** Use software like **Cinebench** or **3DMark** to test CPU and GPU performance.
- **Monitor Temperatures:** Confirm that your cooling setup is functioning and temperatures are within safe ranges.

A Fully Functional System

Installing the OS and configuring drivers is the final step in bringing your PC to life. Whether you choose Windows or Linux, take the time to set everything up correctly to ensure your system runs smoothly. With your new computer ready, you're all set to enjoy the performance and versatility of your custom-built PC!

Chapter 22: Optimization and Maintenance

Once your PC is up and running, you can optimize its performance and keep it in top shape through regular maintenance. Overclocking can unlock additional power, while cooling and cleanliness ensure your system runs efficiently. This chapter will cover the basics of CPU and GPU overclocking, strategies for keeping your PC cool and dust-free, and tips for troubleshooting common problems.

Overclocking Basics for CPU and GPU

Overclocking involves pushing your CPU or GPU beyond its default speed to gain extra performance. While it can yield significant benefits, it requires care to avoid instability or damage.

1. Overclocking Your CPU

Overclocking the CPU increases its clock speed for faster processing, which is especially useful for gaming, rendering, and other demanding tasks.

Steps to Overclock a CPU:

1. **Access the BIOS:**
   - Enter the BIOS during boot by pressing the designated key (e.g., **Delete** or **F2**).
   - Look for overclocking settings under menus like **AI Tweaker, OC,** or **Performance Tuning.**
2. **Increase the Multiplier:**
   - The CPU's clock speed is calculated by multiplying the base clock (usually 100 MHz) by the CPU multiplier.
   - Gradually increase the multiplier to boost the clock speed.
3. **Adjust Voltage:**
   - If your system becomes unstable, slightly increase the CPU voltage (Vcore) to provide more power. Be cautious—too much voltage generates extra heat and risks damage.
4. **Stress Test:**
   - Use tools like **Prime95, Cinebench,** or **AIDA64** to stress test the CPU and check for stability.
   - Monitor temperatures with software like **HWMonitor** or **CoreTemp** to ensure they remain within safe limits (usually below 85°C).

Tips:

- Use an aftermarket cooler to handle the extra heat generated during overclocking.
- Overclock gradually to avoid pushing the CPU beyond its limits.

2. Overclocking Your GPU

Overclocking the GPU improves performance in gaming and graphics-intensive tasks, leading to higher frame rates and smoother visuals.

Steps to Overclock a GPU:

1. **Use Overclocking Software:**
   - Tools like **MSI Afterburner**, **EVGA Precision X1**, or **AMD Radeon Software** allow you to tweak GPU settings easily.
2. **Increase Core Clock Speed:**
   - Gradually raise the core clock speed in increments of 10–20 MHz. Test for stability after each increase using benchmarking tools like **3DMark** or **Heaven Benchmark**.
3. **Adjust Memory Clock Speed:**
   - Similarly, increase the memory clock speed in small increments and test for stability.
4. **Monitor Temperatures:**
   - Keep GPU temperatures below 85°C during stress tests.

Tips:

- Use custom fan curves to improve cooling while overclocking.
- Avoid excessive overclocking that may cause crashes or graphical artifacts.

Keeping Your System Cool and Dust-Free

Proper cooling and cleanliness are essential for maintaining performance and extending the lifespan of your components.

1. Improving Cooling Efficiency

- **Optimize Airflow:** Use a balanced fan setup with intake fans at the front/bottom and exhaust fans at the rear/top.
- **Clean Fans and Filters:** Regularly clean case fans and dust filters to maintain airflow.
- **Reapply Thermal Paste:** Replace thermal paste on your CPU cooler every 2–3 years for optimal heat transfer.
- **Monitor Temperatures:** Use software like **HWMonitor** or **SpeedFan** to track component temperatures and fan speeds.

2. Keeping Dust Out

- **Use Dust Filters:** Install filters over intake vents to block dust from entering the case.
- **Clean Regularly:** Use compressed air to blow dust out of fans, heatsinks, and vents. Avoid using a vacuum, as it can generate static electricity.

- **Elevate Your Case:** Place your case on a flat surface instead of directly on the floor to reduce dust buildup.

3. Cooling Upgrades

- **Add More Fans:** If temperatures remain high, consider adding extra case fans or upgrading to higher-quality models.
- **Switch to Liquid Cooling:** For overclocked or high-performance systems, a liquid cooler (AIO or custom loop) can provide superior cooling.

Tips for Troubleshooting Common Problems

Even with proper assembly and maintenance, issues can arise. Here are common PC problems and how to address them:

1. System Won't Boot

- **Check Power Connections:** Ensure all PSU cables (24-pin ATX, 8-pin CPU, GPU) are securely connected.
- **Verify RAM Placement:** Make sure RAM sticks are properly seated in the correct slots.

- **Clear CMOS:** Reset the BIOS by removing the CMOS battery for a few seconds, then reinserting it.

2. No Display Output

- **Verify Monitor Connection:** Ensure the monitor is connected to the GPU, not the motherboard (unless using integrated graphics).
- **Reseat the GPU:** Remove the GPU and reinsert it into the PCIe slot securely.
- **Test with Another Display or Cable:** Rule out issues with the monitor or HDMI/DisplayPort cable.

3. Overheating

- **Check Fan Operation:** Ensure all fans, including the CPU and GPU fans, are spinning.
- **Improve Airflow:** Rearrange cables and clean dust to enhance cooling.
- **Undervolting:** Reduce component voltages using software to lower heat output without sacrificing performance.

4. Random Crashes or Freezes

- **Check for Driver Updates:** Ensure your GPU and motherboard drivers are up to date.

- **Run Stress Tests:** Use tools like **MemTest86** to test RAM and **Prime95** for the CPU.
- **Scan for Malware:** Run a full scan with antivirus software to rule out malicious programs.

5. Slow Performance

- **Check Background Processes:** Close unnecessary programs in the task manager.
- **Upgrade Storage:** Replace an HDD with an SSD for faster load times and responsiveness.
- **Add More RAM:** If you're running out of memory, consider upgrading your RAM.

Keeping Your PC in Top Shape

Regular maintenance and optimization keep your PC running smoothly and ensure you get the best performance for years to come. By learning the basics of overclocking, keeping your system cool and clean, and troubleshooting issues proactively, you'll maximize the value and longevity of your build. A little effort goes a long way in maintaining a reliable and high-performing machine.

Printed in Great Britain
by Amazon